Technical Writing for Quality

Graham Witt

Technics Publications

Published by:

115 Linda Vista
Sedona, Arizona 86336 USA
https://www.TechnicsPub.com

Edited by Sadie Hoberman

Cover design by Lorena Molinari

All rights reserved. No part of this book may be reproduced or transmitted in any form or by any means, electronic or mechanical, including photocopying, recording or by any information storage and retrieval system, without written permission from the publisher, except for brief quotations in a review.

The author and publisher have taken care in the preparation of this book, but make no expressed or implied warranty of any kind and assume no responsibility for errors or omissions. No liability is assumed for incidental or consequential damages in connection with or arising out of the use of the information or programs contained herein.

All trade and product names are trademarks, registered trademarks, or service marks of their respective companies and are the property of their respective holders and should be treated as such.

First Printing 2023

Copyright © 2023 by Graham Witt

ISBN, print ed.	9781634623551
ISBN, Kindle ed.	9781634623568
ISBN, ePub ed.	9781634623575
ISBN, PDF ed.	9781634623582

Library of Congress Control Number: 2023930976

To my teachers.

Acknowledgments

Although this book is aimed at technical professionals, it is primarily a book about language. My love of language was stimulated early by my grandfather Jack Cade, who gave me copies of Frederick Bodmer's *Loom of Language* and Roget's Thesaurus during my childhood. I have also been privileged to have had some wonderful language teachers over the years: Cornelius O'Neill, who taught me a year's worth of Latin during my first Australian summer so that I could join the High School university stream; and Zorana Popović and Liljana Tasevska, my Serbian and Macedonian teachers respectively.

During my career I have been trusted by colleagues to write a variety of technical material. Graeme Simsion, who launched my consulting career by inviting me to join Simsion Bowles and Associates, trusted me not only to produce documentation for his clients but to co-author the second and third editions of his seminal book *Data Modeling Essentials*. Geoff Howard of Ajilon entrusted me with many responsibilities, including that of negotiating and finalizing the wording of specifications for a multi-governmental IT initiative. David Hayward of Ajilon (later Modis) recalled me from retirement to document in detail the integration of rail operations systems for the Sydney, Australia, metropolitan rail network. Kerrin Paterson then called me out of retirement again to develop data modeling and naming standards (among other things) for a leading Australian university. My thanks to all of you.

To write a book such as this is made so much easier by the support of family and friends – Isabel de Sousa, Brynnin Gilchrist, Gillian Essex, Mark Atkins, and Terry Smith – to all of whom I also owe thanks.

Finally I must thank Steve Hoberman and Lorena Molinari at Technics Publications, who have made the process of writing this book as stress-free as possible. Any errors in this book are my responsibility alone.

Contents at a glance

Chapter 1.	About this book	11
Chapter 2.	Writing for the reader	23
Chapter 3.	Choice of wording	45
Chapter 4.	Specific content	67
Chapter 5.	Typical documents	89
Chapter 6.	Crafting grammatical sentences	109
Chapter 7.	Common errors	157
Chapter 8.	Differences between US and UK Standard English	183
Chapter 9.	The building blocks of English	189

Contents

Chapter 1. About this book 11

   1.1   Why I wrote it (and why you might find it useful) 11

   1.2   The importance of effective communication 11

      1.2.1   Causes and risks of ineffective writing 12

      1.2.2   Why is writing so often ineffective? 12

   1.3   Examples of ineffective communication 15

      1.3.1   Ambiguity 15

      1.3.2   Verbosity 16

      1.3.3   Poor sentence structure 16

   1.4   Scope 17

   1.5   Topics 18

   1.6   How this book is organized 18

   1.7   Caveats 19

   1.8   Conventions adopted in this book 19

   1.9   Abbreviations used in this book 20

Chapter 2. Writing for the reader 23

   2.1   Before you start 23

      2.1.1   Understanding your readers 24

      2.1.2   Register 25

      2.1.3   Style guides 26

      2.1.4   Note taking 28

      2.1.5   Consistency, templates 28

   2.2   Composition and form 29

      2.2.1   Document structure 30

         2.2.1.1   Sections and subsections 30

         2.2.1.2   Paragraphs 31

2.2.2		Sentence clarity	32
2.2.3		Narrative flow	34
	2.2.3.1	Topic and comment	34
	2.2.3.2	Linking phrases	36
2.2.4		Plain English	37
2.2.5		Shortening long sentences	38
2.2.6		Ellipsis	40

2.3 Document layout 41

2.3.1	Spacing	42
2.3.2	Justification	42
2.3.3	Indents	43
2.3.4	Fonts	43
2.3.5	Consistency	43
2.3.6	Tables	44
2.3.7	Emphasis	44

Chapter 3. Choice of wording 45

3.1 The language of the organization 45

3.2 Technical terms 46

3.3 Names 48

3.4 Adjectives 50

3.5 Adverbs 50

3.6 Pronouns and determiners 52

3.7 Facts, opinions, and assumptions 53

3.8 Obligation, capability, prohibition 55

3.9 Words and phrases to avoid 56

3.9.1	Foreign words and phrases	56
3.9.2	Archaic language	57
3.9.3	Buzzwords	58
3.9.4	Headline language	61
3.9.5	Sales and marketing language	62
3.9.6	Weasel words	62

3.9.7	Words with multiple meanings	62
3.9.8	Ambiguous phrases	63
3.9.8.1	Parsing ambiguity	63
3.9.8.2	Ambiguous modals	63
3.9.8.3	Ambiguous expressions of time	64
3.9.9	Double negatives	64
3.9.10	Redundancy	65
3.9.11	Synonyms and contranyms	65
3.9.12	Long noun chains	66
3.9.13	Contractions	66

Chapter 4. Specific content 67

4.1	Series	67
4.2	Definitions	69
4.3	Quoted material	71
4.4	Abbreviations	72
4.4.1	Are abbreviations appropriate?	72
4.4.2	Capitalization and punctuation conventions	73
4.5	Numeric information	74
4.5.1	Dates	75
4.5.2	Times of day	76
4.5.3	Monetary amounts	78
4.5.4	Other quantities	78
4.5.5	Percentages	80
4.5.6	Measurement units	80
4.5.6.1	US units	80
4.5.6.2	International units	81
4.5.7	Numeric identifiers	82
4.5.8	Ordinal numbers	82
4.6	Diagrams	83
4.7	Headings	85
4.8	Cross-references	85

| 4.9 | References to other documents or published works | 86 |
| 4.10 | Front matter | 88 |

Chapter 5. Typical documents 89

5.1 Document lifecycles 89

5.2 Inter-organization documents 90
    5.2.1 Requests for Tenders 90
    5.2.2 Tenders 90
    5.2.3 Contracts 91

5.3 Pre-project documents 91

5.4 Product reviews and recommendations 92

5.5 IT project documents 93
    5.5.1 Requirements specifications 93
    5.5.2 Software specifications 95
        5.5.2.1 Data specifications 95
        5.5.2.2 Process specifications 99
        5.5.2.3 Business rule specifications 100
        5.5.2.4 User interface specifications 102
    5.5.3 Change requests 103
    5.5.4 Release notices 103
    5.5.5 Progress reports 104
    5.5.6 Meeting minutes 104

5.6 Organizational resources 104
    5.6.1 Business glossaries 105
    5.6.2 Standards 105
    5.6.3 User manuals 106
    5.6.4 Standard Operating Procedures 107

5.7 Office communications 107

Chapter 6. Crafting grammatical sentences 109

6.1 Grammatical terms 110
    6.1.1 Word classes 110
    6.1.2 Types of phrases 112

- 6.1.3 Clauses 113
  - 6.1.3.1 Components of a clause 115
  - 6.1.3.2 Transitive and intransitive verbs 116
  - 6.1.3.3 Relative clauses 117
  - 6.1.3.4 Clause scope 118

6.2 Rules of grammar 118
- 6.2.1 Sentence completeness 119
- 6.2.2 Word order 120
  - 6.2.2.1 Subject, verb, and objects 120
  - 6.2.2.2 Adjectives 121
  - 6.2.2.3 Verb phrases 123
  - 6.2.2.4 Phrasal verbs 123
  - 6.2.2.5 Adverb phrases 124
  - 6.2.2.6 Determiners 126
  - 6.2.2.7 Prepositional phrases 126
- 6.2.3 Conjoined clauses 126
  - 6.2.3.1 Conjunction behavior 127
  - 6.2.3.2 Conjunctions and nonfinite verb phrases 128
  - 6.2.3.3 Conjunction semantics 129
- 6.2.4 Subject-verb agreement 129
- 6.2.5 Determiner-noun agreement 131
- 6.2.6 Pronoun rules 133
- 6.2.7 Preposition rules 134
- 6.2.8 Comparative and superlative adjectives 135

6.3 Contentious rules 135
- 6.3.1 Splitting the infinitive 135
- 6.3.2 Ending a sentence with a preposition 136
- 6.3.3 Using the passive voice 136
- 6.3.4 The Oxford comma 137

6.4 Rules governing series 138
- 6.4.1 Consistency 138
- 6.4.2 Conjunction use 139
- 6.4.3 Series Punctuation 139

6.5 Indefinite articles 140

6.6	Forming the possessive of a long compound noun	141
6.7	**Punctuation**	**141**
6.7.1	Periods / full stops	141
6.7.2	Commas	142
6.7.3	Colons	145
6.7.4	Semicolons	146
6.7.5	Parentheses	146
6.7.6	Square brackets	147
6.7.7	Dashes	147
6.7.8	Ellipses	148
6.7.9	Quotation marks	148
6.7.10	Obliques	149
6.7.11	Apostrophes	149
6.7.12	Hyphens	150
6.7.13	Question and exclamation marks	151
6.7.14	Periods, commas, and quotation marks	151
6.7.15	Punctuation and spaces	152
6.8	**Capitalization**	**153**
6.8.1	Names	153
6.8.2	Headings	153
6.8.3	Specific and generic instances	154
6.8.4	Other capitalization rules	155

Chapter 7. Common errors 157

7.1	**Ambiguity**	**157**
7.1.1	Pronouns	157
7.1.2	Prepositional phrases that may apply to more than one noun phrase	158
7.1.3	Words and phrases with multiple meanings	158
7.1.4	Syntactic ambiguity	159
7.1.5	Temporal ambiguity	159
7.1.6	Other sources of ambiguity	160
7.2	**Word order**	**161**
7.2.1	Dangling modifiers	161
7.2.2	Misplaced modifiers	162
7.2.3	Separation of related phrases	163

	7.2.4	Subject-verb reversal in indirect questions	164
7.3		Confusing singular and plural	164
7.4		Plural noun phrases	164
7.5		Misuse of determiners	165
7.6		Incomplete sentences	167
7.7		Confusing objects and their names	167
7.8		Imprecise terminology	167
7.9		Term overload	168
7.10		Incorrect prepositions	169
7.11		Confusing adjectives and adverbs	169
7.12		Breaking chronological order	169
7.13		Using the wrong conjunction	169
	7.13.1	At the start of a relative clause	169
	7.13.2	In a series	170
7.14		Errors in usage	170
	7.14.1	Commonly confused words, abbreviations, and phrases	170
	7.14.2	Similar but distinct phrases	173
	7.14.3	Plurals often used wrongly	174
	7.14.4	Words, phrases, and clauses often used wrongly	174
	7.14.5	Common misspellings	175
	7.14.6	Nonexistent words	176
	7.14.7	Confusion between plural and possessive	176
7.15		Verbosity	176
	7.15.1	Superfluous words	176
	7.15.2	Repetition	177
	7.15.3	Unwieldy sentences	177
7.16		Punctuation errors	178

Chapter 8.   Differences between US and UK Standard English *183*

8.1	Vocabulary	183
8.2	Spelling	184
8.3	Phrases	186
8.4	Dates	187
8.5	Punctuation	187
8.6	Personal Names	188
8.7	Title case	188

Chapter 9. The building blocks of English 189

9.1	Nouns	189
9.1.1	Possessives	190
9.1.2	Compound nouns	190
9.1.3	Gerunds	192
9.1.4	Plurals	192
9.1.4.1	Mutating plurals	192
9.1.4.2	Foreign plurals	192
9.1.4.3	Irregular plurals	193
9.1.4.4	Unmarked plurals	194
9.1.4.5	Regular plurals	194
9.1.4.6	Nouns without plurals	195
9.1.4.7	Nouns without a singular form	196
9.1.5	Proper Nouns	196
9.2	Determiners	197
9.3	Adjectives	198
9.3.1	Compound adjectives	198
9.3.2	Gerundives and past participles	198
9.3.3	Ordinal numbers	198
9.3.4	Comparative and superlative adjectives	199
9.4	Pronouns	199
9.5	Prepositions	202
9.6	Verbs	204

9.6.1	Verb forms		205
9.6.2	Irregular verbs		207
9.6.3	Tenses		210
	9.6.3.1	Simple present	210
	9.6.3.2	Simple future	210
	9.6.3.3	Simple past	211
	9.6.3.4	Perfect tenses	211
	9.6.3.5	Progressive tenses	212
	9.6.3.6	Other tense-like verb constructions	213
9.6.4	Active and passive voice		213
9.6.5	Negation		214
9.6.6	Mood		215
	9.6.6.1	Interrogative mood	215
	9.6.6.2	Imperative mood	216
	9.6.6.3	Subjunctive mood	217
9.6.7	Primary auxiliaries		217
9.6.8	Modals		218
	9.6.8.1	Can, could	218
	9.6.8.2	May, might	219
	9.6.8.3	Must	219
	9.6.8.4	Shall, should	220
	9.6.8.5	Will, would	220
9.6.9	Semi-modal verbs		220
	9.6.9.1	Dare	221
	9.6.9.2	Need	221
	9.6.9.3	Ought to	221
	9.6.9.4	Used to	221
9.6.10	Phrasal verbs		222
9.6.11	Verbs before "that", "if", "whether", or "to"		222
9.6.12	Verbs before clauses		223

9.7 Conjunctions 223

9.7.1 Coordinating conjunctions..223
9.7.2 Subordinating conjunctions..223

9.8 Adverbs 224

9.9 Phrases 225

9.9.1	Noun phrases	226
9.9.2	Finite verb phrases	227
9.9.3	Nonfinite verb phrases	228
9.9.3.1	Present participial phrases	228
9.9.3.2	Past participial phrases	229
9.9.3.3	Infinitive phrases	229
9.9.4	Adjective phrases	229
9.9.5	Adverb phrases	230
9.9.6	Prepositional phrases	231
9.9.7	Absolute phrases	231
9.9.8	Combining phrases using logical conjunctions	231
9.9.8.1	Combining verb phrases	232
9.9.8.2	Combining attributive adjective phrases	233

Chapter 1. About this book

1.1 Why I wrote it (and why you might find it useful)

Having worked in IT for five decades in many roles, I have spent much of that time writing or reviewing not only code, models, and databases but documents. These include tenders, recommendations, business glossaries, requirements specifications, user manuals, and standards documents. When such documents have been understandable and unambiguous, the activities supported by those documents have been effective and efficient, but all too often, where documents are unclear or ambiguous, costly time-consuming rework has been required.

While IT projects involve modeling and coding, both forms of human-machine communication, a major contribution to the success of a project is the quality of human-human communication, both orally and in writing. This book is for anyone who wants to communicate more effectively when writing in the English language. Its primary target audience is IT professionals who need to document what they do for the benefit of others. It may also be of value to professionals in other fields.

1.2 The importance of effective communication

Every IT professional needs to communicate with colleagues, clients and other human beings using a common language, even if only in the form of data definitions, process descriptions or business rules. Many need to write formal documents as part of the documentation of a new system or data resource.

The purpose of written communication is to express assertions or questions in a manner that the reader understands. Written communication involves the writer visualizing a set of related mental concepts and translating it into a natural language, which the reader then translates into their own mental picture.

Communication is only effective when the reader creates the same concepts and relationships as the writer. If the reader is (a) unable to create any meaningful concepts and relationships, or (b) creates concepts and relationships that differ from those of the writer, communication has broken down.

1.2.1 Causes and risks of ineffective writing

Writing may be ineffective for several reasons. Ambiguity makes writing less understandable, as do poor document organization, poor sentence structure, unclear argument, verbosity, and inappropriate word usage. A document with any of these failings lacks clarity: it is difficult to understand and therefore poses risks to the organization using it. For example:

- in requirements, lack of clarity may lead to acquisition of a system lacking required features or may lead to money or effort being expended on unnecessary features.
- in system specifications, lack of clarity may lead to rework, increasing the acquisition cost and timeline.

1.2.2 Why is writing so often ineffective?

As a student in England and Australia in the 50s and 60s, I was taught grammar, but as a teacher in the late 60s, I discovered that "self-expression" had replaced grammar in the curriculum. I then worked in a variety of organizations in which management, schooled in English usage rules, expected documents to follow those rules.

However, in many of the documents I have reviewed in my IT career, I have repeatedly observed the same issues, in particular:

- overlong sentences[1], resulting from either too many ideas crammed into the one sentence or the inclusion of superfluous words that added nothing useful
- poorly structured sentences[2], often resulting from adding at the end of a sentence words that should have been included elsewhere in the sentence
- the use of words like the one the writer most likely had in mind — but unfortunately the wrong word for the occasion[3]
- circuitous arguments, in which the writer has obviously struggled with multiple options and their advantages and disadvantages but has not set these out clearly
- ungrammatical sentences.

These issues seem to arise from both psychological and technological causes:

- **Overlong sentences** may result from a desire to impress or uncertainty about the subject matter.
- **Poorly structured** sentences may result if the writer puts down ideas as they occur without then reading each sentence or paragraph to see if it can be improved.
- A wrong word, produced by either the writer or autocorrect, may be included if the writer believes it to be the right word, which in turn may be due to unwarranted confidence on the part of the writer.

---

[1] Section 1.3.2 includes some examples.
[2] Section 1.3.3 includes some examples.
[3] Section 7.14.1 lists some commonly confused words.

- A circuitous argument may result if the writer has not stepped back from it, organized their thoughts, then committed them to the document. It is best to organize thoughts on a whiteboard in a tabular or graphical form.
- An ungrammatical sentence may result if the writer relies too much on their word processor's editing feature. While these have improved over time, the suggestions they make may still be inappropriate. For example, the Word 365 editing feature suggested the following improvements on phrases in this book:
    - "a standard document" instead of "a standards document"
    - "added terms", "unfamiliar terms", or "updated terms", none of which are appropriate alternatives, instead of "new terms"
    - "don't use a pronoun" instead of "do not use a pronoun"
    - "staff" instead of "employees"[4]
    - *"use only pronoun"[5] instead of "only use a pronoun".

Today, people obtain information from multiple sources:

- Dictionaries, being descriptive rather than prescriptive, include words and meanings that are in common use, often with little or no indication of their acceptability in technical writing.
- Several websites claim to check grammar, yet many of these give inappropriate advice.
- Much of the language on social media platforms is unsuitable for technical writing, but it has become part of a social media user's language environment.

---

[4] When I changed "employees" to "staff", it then suggested I change "staff" to "employees".

[5] Syntactically incorrect constructions are conventionally indicated by way of an initial asterisk.

1.3 Examples of ineffective communication

Ambiguity, verbosity, and poor sentence structure are arguably the three most common causes of ineffective communication.

1.3.1 Ambiguity

If an assertion or question may be interpreted in more than one way, the reader may realize this and try to work out which interpretation was intended; with luck, the intended interpretation might be guessed. However, if the reader must pause to choose an interpretation, that distraction will dilute the writer's message. Moreover, the reader may choose a different interpretation from the one intended: communication has then broken down. Oral communication lets the listener seek clarification, but with written communication there may be no opportunity for clarification.

Consider the following sentences:

- !"There have been requests for this restriction to be removed from both the New York and London offices."[6]
  Have the requests come from those offices, or have they requested removal of restrictions from those offices?

- !"Despite initial differences of opinion between the Data Modeler and the Database Administrator, he eventually acquiesced to enforcement of all constraints after each load."
  Did the Data Modeler or the Database Administrator acquiesce?

- !"The project manager agreed to finish the project."
  Did the manager agree to an immediate cessation of the project, or to it being continued until complete?

---

[6] Any text that is grammatical but not recommended is preceded by an exclamation mark.

- !"Uniqueness constraints may govern one column or multiple columns."
  Does this mean that there may be one or more single-column constraints, each on a different column, or that there may be multi-column constraints?
- !"He had classified documents."
  Was he in possession of documents that had a security classification, or had he classified some documents?

Section 7.1 discusses how to remove ambiguity from sentences.

1.3.2 Verbosity

Some documents use more words than necessary to make the point. This also inhibits effective communication, as it requires the reader to wade through convoluted sentences trying to deduce what is meant. Consider the following sentences:

- !"Taking into consideration the requirements of the Department, the identification of which was the objective of the workshops conducted as part of this project, and the capabilities and functionality of the software products which were included in the shortlist agreed with the Department, evaluation of those products against those requirements was conducted, the results of which form the content of this report, it being a contractual deliverable."
- !"For those functions which are listed in the Requirements Specification for this project and for which successful execution was unable to be achieved, the support service provided by the shortlisted vendor was contacted, leading to either advice from the vendor as to how to achieve successful execution or to advice that the function would form part of a subsequent release or would not."

Section 7.15.3 discusses how to edit these sentences to be easier to understand.

1.3.3 Poor sentence structure

This is yet another barrier to effective communication, as it requires the reader to reconstruct what was meant. Consider the following sentences:

- !"The same sample model was loaded into each candidate software product provided by the Department."
  This suggests that the software products (rather than the sample model) were provided by the Department.
- !"It was later established that the modifications included were inappropriate by Mr. Smith."
  Did Smith establish that the modifications were inappropriate, or was he the person who included those modifications?

Section 7.2.2 discusses how to make these sentences easier to understand.

1.4   Scope

As the title of this book implies, its focus is technical writing, covering:

- documents created to support the development of IT assets, such as project proposals, business cases, recommendations, requirements specifications, business glossaries, software specifications (data specifications, process specifications, business rule specifications), user manuals, and IT policy documents
- documents created for communication between different organizations, such as requests for tenders, tenders, and contracts.

However, since IT projects inevitably involve intraoffice communications, such as e-mails, memoranda, and progress reports, I have included some discussion of those too.

US and UK English usages differ in various ways.[7] As this book is published in the US, it conforms to US conventions, but where US and UK usages differ, both usages are provided. This book will therefore meet the needs of writers in

---

[7] Chapter 8 details the differences.

English in British Commonwealth countries and the European Union (particularly Ireland) as well as the US.

1.5 Topics

In this book you will find:

- practical techniques for the creation of documents that can be easily understood by readers and that accurately convey the intended message
- practical advice on document organization and layout
- discussion of the rules and conventions that govern expression in the English language
- examples of easy mistakes that may be made when writing in English together with corrected alternatives
- a comparison of the US and UK variants of English
- a ready reference to dip into while creating a written document.

1.6 How this book is organized

Part 1 focuses on the craft of technical document writing:

- Chapter 2 describes how to produce documents that engage and inform readers.
- Chapter 3 discusses the importance of choosing appropriate words and phrases.
- Chapter 4 covers specific types of content requiring considerations that go beyond grammar.
- Chapter 5 covers typical documents that an IT professional might produce, and guidelines for doing so.
- Chapter 6 describes the grammatical and other rules which should be followed when writing a technical or business document.
- Chapter 7 lists some common errors made by writers.

Part 2 provides detailed reference material:

- Chapter 8 covers differences between US and UK English.
- Chapter 9 defines and provides examples of each word class and each type of phrase and describes how certain words change in different contexts.

1.7 Caveats

Two features of the English language could make a book such as this hard to write and read. First, there are many rules, most of which have exceptions. Second, there are many ways to construct sentences. Given these features, I have described only a subset of the language, but one which I believe covers the needs of a technical writer. For example, none of the lists of example words and phrases included in this book is guaranteed to be exhaustive.

1.8 Conventions adopted in this book

In this book:

- **Bold serif** is used for technical terms, where first used in a section, and elsewhere as appropriate.
- Sans serif on a grey background is used for examples of words, phrases, clauses, or sentences (whether recommended or not):
  - each ungrammatical example is preceded by the symbol '*'
  - each example that is grammatical but not recommended is preceded by the symbol '!'.
- The symbols '<' and '>' enclosing a term indicate that any instance of that term may be used, for example '<adverb> <adjective>' means that any adverb may be used followed by any adjective.

1.9 Abbreviations used in this book

This book uses the following abbreviations:

- CIO: Chief Information Officer
- DBMS: Database Management System
- EU: European Union
- ISO: International Organization for Standardization
- IT: Information Technology
- SQL: Structured Query Language
- UK: United Kingdom
- US: United States

Part 1: Crafting effective documents

Chapter 2. Writing for the reader

If a document is to be effective, the writer must be clear about two things:

- the purpose of the document, in terms of what outcomes the document is to support, for example:
    - The purpose of a requirements specification is to ensure that data and process modelers create models from which developers can build a system that meets the specified requirements.
    - The purpose of a data specification is to enable appropriate team members to either build a database or understand its structure.
    - The purpose of a release notice is to ensure that system users understand the differences in behavior and usage of the new release compared with the previous release.
- the audience:
    - who is going to read the document
    - why they might read it
    - what each of them already knows about the topic(s) presented
    - how each of them is likely to obtain information from the document.

The principal focus of this chapter is those aspects of a document that will assist readers' understanding, such as its overall structure, the clarity of sentences, and narrative flow. Before that, however, it proposes some useful activities to help the writer prepare for writing a document, mainly understanding its readers.

2.1   Before you start

Before starting on a document, you should ask—and obtain answers to—the following questions:

- What is the purpose of this document? What outcomes do we expect from its publication?

- Who is going to read it?
- Why are they going to read it?
- What does each reader already know about the topic(s) presented?
- How is each reader likely to obtain information from the document?

The answers to these questions should guide the writing process in terms of composition, choice of words, and so on.

2.1.1 Understanding your readers

There are three ways in which readers obtain information from a document:

- **sequential**: starting at the beginning and reading to the end; this may involve skipping material that is not relevant to the reader's needs
- **selective**: consulting the table of contents and deciding which chapters or sections are worth reading
- **random**: typically used when consulting a reference document: looking up a term of interest in the table of contents or index, then reading the appropriate section(s) in depth.

If the recipients of a document are likely to use different reading strategies, the writer must take care to cater for them all, particularly regarding the use and definition of technical terms and abbreviations. For example, if the writer includes a technical term toward the end of a document which has been defined at the start, some readers may encounter it having either (a) not read the definition or (b) read it but forgotten it, particularly if the document is long or includes many technical terms. Section 4.2 discusses techniques for assisting such readers.

Whichever strategy a given reader employs, their understanding of material in a document will be informed by (a) what has preceded that material, and n(b) what they already know, believe, or assume about the topic.

Another factor that may affect readers' understanding is whether they will remain motivated working through a document of any length. One thing that demotivates readers is having to wade through many pages of detail before getting a sense of why they are reading the document (and whether they should be). To gain and keep reader interest:

- Include at the start of the document a concise introduction that summarizes the purpose and content of the document. This lets readers know (a) why they should read it, and (b) what they should do with the information.
- Move any lengthy detailed material (such as a glossary) to the end of the document. Advise readers that there is a glossary or other detailed material, by including in the introduction a guide to the organization of document content.
- Provide specific facts and concrete examples rather than generalizations or abstract statements. If a general or abstract statement is necessary, follow it with specific facts and/or concrete examples. For example, if a project proposal includes a statement such as "this enhancement will provide a simpler means of identifying customers to be targeted with offers", this should be followed by details of how the enhanced system differs from the current system.
- Distinguish clearly between established facts, opinions, and assumptions, as described in Section 3.7.

2.1.2 Register

Register refers to variation in language to suit the purpose or situation. Register may be classified as **formal**, **standard**, and **informal**. Compare the following possible introductions to a software user manual:

- **formal**: "So that we maximize our investment in this new software package, it is incumbent on all personnel whose duties require that they use it to familiarize themselves with all relevant functionality."

- **standard**: "All staff who use the new software will have a more rewarding experience if they understand the best ways to use it."
- **informal**: "Since you'll be using this software, let's get a handle on it."

Formal language creates distance between the writer and reader, which may demotivate the reader. On the other hand, informal language, while appropriate for social communication, may lead the reader not to take a document seriously. The standard register is almost always the most appropriate register to use in technical writing.

Register also varies within the organizational environment: emails and other interoffice communication may be less formal than training material, which may be less formal than procedure manuals, which may in turn be less formal than specifications, while inter-organization documents such as contracts require the most formality.

A standard register is achieved by using:

- established words rather than slang, dialect, or newly coined words
- standard grammatical structures rather than dialect forms
- full words rather than **contractions**, such as "can't", "it'll", and "we'd".

2.1.3 Style guides

Each country in which English is an official language uses at least one **style guide**. These set out rules governing such elements of writing as plain language; choice of words in particular contexts; spelling; abbreviations; punctuation; capitalization; citations; and formatting of numbers, measurements, and dates.

The *Suggested Reading* list at the end of this book lists guides from Australia, Canada, the EU, South Africa, the UK, and the US.

Which guide should the writer follow? A large company or government body may have its own guide, in which case anyone writing a document for that organization should follow that guide. If the organization has no style guide, the choice of guide depends on:

- whether the organization is multinational
- whether the project for which the documentation is being produced is being run in one or more than one country
- whether any technology or software acquired through that project will be used in one or more than one country
- how many official style guides there are in the relevant country or countries.

If the organization only operates in one country and that country only uses one official guide, that is the guide to follow.

However, if that country uses more than one official guide, the writer should find out which one the organization follows. If the organization has not yet chosen a guide, the writer should choose one, follow it, and include in each document a statement identifying the chosen style guide. This is so that, if the organization later chooses a different guide, documents can, if necessary, be more easily edited in line with the chosen guide.

If the organization operates in more than one country, the choice of guide should be based on (a) the country or countries in which the project is being run, (b) organization policy on international projects, and (c) which country or countries any software acquired through that project will be used in. Although the answers to those questions may determine a single style guide, a project producing software to be used in more than one country may have to produce multiple versions of user manuals.

The writer should establish which guide to follow before starting serious work on a document, although they can take notes while that is being established.

2.1.4   Note taking

A useful aid to crafting an effective document is a separate, informal document in which the writer keeps notes about such aspects as:

- recipients (including those who will review, approve, and endorse the document): their names, position titles, and any expectations
- the overall structure, and the topics to cover
- reminders of essential information to include, before having established what to say and where
- reminders of checks to be made on the accuracy of statements
- resequencing of content
- business-specific and technical terminology.

2.1.5   Consistency, templates

One of the most important characteristics of a quality document is consistency in spelling, grammar, layout, and appearance. Basing a document on a well-designed document template reduces the effort required to achieve consistency. The writer, therefore, needs to establish whether the organization uses such a template.

However, in my experience, too many organizations seem to have given the task of building their standard template to someone with no idea about consistent layout or template features. The most common error is to leave the default language as US English even if the organization is based outside the US. Setting the default language to the appropriate variant of English means that spelling and grammar checking correctly reject nonstandard writing (spelling, phrasing, and punctuation) and accept standard writing. This can be done within a document without changing its appearance.

Another common error is inconsistent or illogical indenting and vertical spacing. Correcting these settings to comply with the guidelines in Section 2.3 will make subsequent documents inconsistent with any existing documents, so negotiation will be necessary, most likely resulting in a compromise.

If there is no standard organization template, you can create one, setting:

- the appropriate language variant
- paragraph styles for headings at each level, body text, table headers and other content, captions for tables and figures, footnotes, and page headers and footers, each with:
    - indenting, vertical spacing before and after the paragraph, and line spacing within the paragraph
    - fonts and character sizes
- character styles for special nonstandard text within body text, such as emphasized words or programming language extracts
- standard "boilerplate" text such as **front matter**[8].

2.2   Composition and form

A reader of a document will better understand it if (a) there is a logical overall structure to the document, and (b) each sentence is clear in its meaning.

---

[8] See Section 4.10.

2.2.1 Document structure

A document of any length should be broken into sections and subsections, with the sentences in each (sub)section collected into paragraphs.

2.2.1.1 Sections and subsections

Any document of more than a few pages should include:

- an introductory section providing information such as a context for the document, its purpose, and its scope (what it covers and, just as important, what it does not cover)
- a closing section listing conclusions and/or recommendations
- additional sections between the introductory and closing sections; these will vary by document type, for example:
    - in an internal recommendations document: sections discussing requirements and options for meeting those requirements (in that sequence)
    - in a recommendations document produced by an external consultant: sections on research methods and sources, findings, and discussion of the implications of those findings
    - in a technical standards document: a section listing the processes or types of artifacts covered by the standards, followed by a separate section for each process or type of artifact
    - in a data specification for review by business stakeholders, a section listing the business concepts (entity classes), followed by a separate section for each entity class listing its attributes and business rules
    - in a data specification for a relational or object-relational database, a section listing the tables, followed by a separate section for each table listing its columns and constraints.

Each section typically has subsections, for example:

- In a technical standards document, each artifact type might have structural standards governing its composition and standards governing the names of the components.
- In a data specification, the sections for each entity class might be grouped by subject area (such as customers, products, and orders).

The sequencing of sections and subsections is important. Alternative approaches to overall sequencing are:

- **inductive**: introduction[9], details, conclusion
- **deductive**: proposition, supporting arguments.

Within a section, detailed discussion of a topic should follow general discussion of that topic. In documents dealing with events over time (such as a project proposal), use a chronological sequence.

In a section with many subsections, including an introductory subsection at the start and/or a summary subsection at the end may be helpful to the reader.

Each section and subsection should have a heading. Section 4.7 covers headings in detail.

2.2.1.2 Paragraphs

The sentences in a section or subsection should be organized into separate paragraphs. Start a new paragraph when the narrative switches to a new topic, issue, or perspective.

---

[9] Often labeled "Executive Summary".

Some studies suggest that the optimum length for a paragraph is from three to five sentences, whereas others set a maximum of eight lines. Occasional shorter paragraphs are acceptable; in particular, a **bulleted** or **numbered list**[10] consists of individual paragraphs for each list item.

2.2.2 Sentence clarity

A reader will understand a sentence more easily if:

- it consists of words which are familiar to the reader
- any unfamiliar words in the sentence are defined (either in the sentence itself or elsewhere via a **cross-reference**[11])
- it relates clearly to previous material (narrative flow)
- it is logically arranged
- it conforms to the grammatical rules of English
- it is concise (no longer than necessary to convey the intended message).

Each of these aspects is discussed in this book: choice of words in Chapter 3, definitions in Section 4.2, narrative flow in Section 2.2.3, sentence arrangement in Section 6.2.2, and grammatical rules in Section 6.2.

As for conciseness, there is a consensus that readers can understand shorter sentences more easily than longer ones. Recommendations vary as to what is too long, but most agree that writers should aim to keep each sentence to under about twenty words. Section 2.2.5 discusses techniques for shortening long sentences, including breaking them into shorter ones.

---

[10] See Section 4.1.

[11] Section 4.8 discusses cross-references.

However, the **readability** of a sentence (the ease with which the average reader can understand it) depends more on the number of syllables than the number of words. If the writer uses shorter words, they may use more of them in a sentence before having to break it apart. The ultimate test of sentence length is whether the average reader can read the sentence once and understand it.

There are standard readability formulae, many of which[12] produce a grade level as defined by the US education system, which may be difficult to interpret. Alternatively, the Flesch-Kincaid formula (available with Microsoft Word 365) yields a score between 1 and 100. The higher the score, the more readable the text.

Sentences may be too short. Occasional short sentences are fine, but an unbroken sequence of consecutive short sentences would be monotonous, and even irritating, especially if all sentences have the same form. Consider the sentences in Figure 1.

> This platform copes with high data volumes. It accommodates many data types. It supports many simultaneous users. It supports complex queries. It returns query results quickly.

Figure 1: A sequence of short sentences

If it is essential to list the platform's features, two alternatives would be more appropriate: (a) a **bulleted** or **numbered list**[13], or (b) two longer sentences, each listing a set of related features. Figure 2 illustrates both alternatives.

---

[12] Including the Gunning-Fog Score, Coleman-Liau Index, SMOG Index, and Automated Readability Index.

[13] These are both described in Section 4.1.

This platform: • copes with high data volumes • accommodates many data types • supports many simultaneous users • supports complex queries • returns query results quickly.	This high-performance platform copes with high data volumes, supports many simultaneous users, and returns query results quickly. It is also flexible, supporting many data types and complex queries.

Figure 2: Alternatives to a sequence of short sentences

2.2.3 Narrative flow

It is important that each sentence relates clearly to previous material. Readers should be able to recognize in each sentence both (a) something with which they are familiar, and (b) information that is new.

Consider the sentence "Primary and foreign keys are essential if data quality is to be maintained." If the reader is a data modeler, they should be familiar with the concepts of primary and foreign keys but not necessarily with the concept of data quality. If the reader is someone for whom data quality is important, they may not be familiar with primary and foreign keys.

Of course, there may be readers familiar with neither of those concepts: if that is likely, the document should introduce one of those concepts before including the above sentence.

If you wish to include additional information about something being discussed but are not sure that all readers may need or be interested in that additional information, include it in a footnote. The list of readability formulae in the previous section is an example of such information.

2.2.3.1 Topic and comment

The **topic** (or **theme**) of a sentence is the subject matter, whereas the **comment** (or **focus**) is new information about the subject matter. In the clause "this column contains only positive integers", the topic is "This column". For this sentence to make any sense, it should be clear to the reader from a previous sentence which column this sentence refers to. The comment "contains only positive integers" provides information about the topic, information that will be new to at least some readers.

The topic of the above sentence is also the **subject** of that sentence, but a sentence may have a topic other than the subject, as in "In this table, every column must have a value in every row." Here the topic is "this table" whereas the subject is "every column". The sentence will only make sense if the preceding material has identified a particular table.

The topic of the sentence "Given the high volumes of data, integrity checking will be disabled during data loading." is "the high volumes of data" whereas the subject is "integrity checking". In this case, if readers are likely to already know that there are high data volumes before reading the document, the preceding material may not need to refer to it.

2.2.3.2 Linking phrases

A **linking phrase** assists the reader in establishing the relationship of a sentence to the preceding sentence(s). Table 1 lists some examples.

Purpose of sentence	Linking phrases
additional detail	In particular,
further argument supporting a proposition	In addition, Moreover,
example(s)	For example, For instance,
implication	As a result, Consequently, For this reason, Given this, In view of this, Therefore, From this we can infer that It follows that
sequence	Next, Subsequently,
contrast	Alternatively, By contrast, However, Instead, Despite this, Even so,
additional example(s), similar situations	Similarly, Meanwhile,
statement of frequency of something	Often, Rarely, All too often,
statement of timescale of something	Today, These days, Previously, In future,
statement of success criteria	To be effective,

Table 1: Linking phrases

Only use the phrases "In view of this", "Given this", or "Despite this" if "this" clearly refers to only one thing in the previous sentence, as in "The previous development cycle failed to deliver all promised enhancements. Given this, we have decided to reduce the number of enhancements in the current cycle." Alternatively, follow "this" with a **noun phrase** to make clear what is meant, as in "Data integrity checks should be run after each load. Despite this requirement, data quality continues to deteriorate."

A linking phrase may contain specific detail, as in the following examples:

- "By contrast with earlier projects,"
- "Having completed testing,"
- "In the event of a communications failure,"
- "When logging out,"
- "As a precaution,"
- "As well as optimizing data loads,"
- "In all cases other than this one,"
- "Before closing the application,"
- "To ensure compliance,"
- "As requirement #137 implies,".

Section 3.7 lists some linking phrases that may be used when expressing opinions or assumptions rather than proven facts.

2.2.4 Plain English

In 1948, the UK government asked Sir Ernest Gowers, a senior civil servant, to create a guide to writing in a more understandable manner than that used by government bodies in official communication. *The Complete Plain Words*, first published in 1954, is still in print. Even though Gowers argued that legal English was a special case, there has also been a trend toward plainer language in legal documents.

Similarly, after earlier moves toward plain language in government writing, the US federal government Plain Writing Act of 2010 made plain language a federal requirement of government departments.

A key message of this initiative is that a writer can often use fewer words to convey the same message.

2.2.5 Shortening long sentences

There are various techniques you can employ to shorten a sentence that is too long:

- Remove unnecessary words, as in the examples in Section 7.15.1.
- Use shorter expressions, such as:
    - "because" rather than "as a consequence of"
    - "now" or "currently" rather than "at this point in time"
    - "reclassify" rather than "change the classification of"
    - "redefine" rather than "change the definition of"
    - "redirect" rather than "change the direction of"
    - "aware of" rather than "cognizant of"
    - "conclude that" rather than "come to the conclusion that"
    - "on detecting" rather than "following the detection of"
    - "consider" rather than "give consideration to"
    - "advise" rather than "give advice to"
    - "discuss" rather than "have a conversation"
    - "about", "concerning", or "regarding" rather than "in relation to", "in respect of", "in regard to", "in connection with", "in the case of", or "with respect to"
    - "equals" rather than "is equal to"
    - "avoids" rather than "is for the avoidance of"
    - "we have noticed" rather than "it has come to our attention"
    - "approach" rather than "make an approach to"

- - "support" rather than "provide support for"
  - "over" rather than "upwards of"
- Use shorter words, such as:
  - "expect" rather than "anticipate"
  - "start" rather than "commence"
  - "use" rather than "utilize".
- If a sentence has two **clauses** joined by "and", "or", "but", "because", or "so", split it into two sentences: replace the conjunction between the clauses by an **adverb phrase** at the start of the second resulting sentence. For example,
  "The majority of requested enhancements have been included in the forthcoming release due in late November, but two enhancements, namely real-time schedule adjustment and crew reassignment, are deferred to the following release due early next year."
  may be recast as
  "The majority of requested enhancements have been included in the forthcoming release due in late November. However, two enhancements, namely real-time schedule adjustment and crew reassignment, are deferred to the following release due early next year."
  Here, "but" has been replaced by "However,".
  Other **conjunctions** can be replaced as follows:
  - "and" by "Also,", "Moreover," or "In addition,"
  - "or" with "Alternatively,"
  - "because" with "This is because"
  - "so" with "Therefore," or "As a result,".
- A sentence with **main** and **dependent clauses** can be split if it is too long. For example,
  "If validation checks fail after the load of the previous day's data, the column with invalid data should be loaded with an appropriate value in each invalid row, a report listing all invalid rows should be emailed to the data steward, and the data steward should immediately undertake data remediation."
  may be recast as
  "If validation checks fail after the load of the previous day's data, a remediation process occurs. This involves (a) the column with invalid data being loaded with an appropriate value in each invalid row, (b) a report listing all invalid rows

being emailed to the data steward, and (c) the data steward immediately undertaking data remediation."

- If the sentence contains an **inline series**, convert it to a **bulleted** or **numbered list**[14]. For example,
  "This involves (a) the column with invalid data being loaded with an appropriate value in each invalid row, (b) a report listing all invalid rows being emailed to the data steward, and (c) the data steward immediately undertaking data remediation."
  may be recast as
  "This involves:
    o the column with invalid data being loaded with an appropriate value in each invalid row
    o a report listing all invalid rows being emailed to the data steward, and
    o the data steward immediately undertaking data remediation."

- **Ellipsis** can be used to remove repeated content, as described in the next section.

2.2.6   Ellipsis

The sentence "We have tested all functions, and we have prepared a report listing test results." consists of two **independent clauses** with the same **subject** ("we"). When this occurs, we may omit the subject from the second clause, in this case yielding "We have tested all functions, and have prepared a report listing test results." We may even omit the repeated "have", to yield "We have tested all functions, and prepared a report listing test results."

This omission of repeated content is known as **ellipsis**. Other examples are:

- "This is the most comprehensive package of this type that is or has been available." ("available" is understood after "that is")

---

[14] See Section 4.1.

- "This report details our long- and short-term plans."

Make sure that the omitted content makes sense if reinserted. Consider *"The database's purpose is to support business intelligence and is therefore optimized."[15] The **subject** has been omitted from the second clause, but the subject of the first clause is "the database's purpose": inserting that subject into the second clause yields *"The database's purpose is therefore optimized." when presumably what is intended is "The database is therefore optimized."

Another error resulting from ellipsis may occur when part of a **compound noun** is omitted. Consider "Both the development team and the test team will participate in testing." Removing just the first "team" but retaining the second "the" yields *"Both the development and the test team will participate in testing." which suggests that one of the testing participants will be "the development". Correct ellipsis would yield "Both the development and test teams will participate in testing."

2.3 Document layout

A document with a consistent layout is more readable, as it introduces fewer distractions.

To avoid the document looking crowded, create white space by:

- splitting long paragraphs
- increasing all margins to at least 1" (2.5 cm)
- increasing **vertical spacing** (particularly the spacing above each paragraph) to at least 10 point for plain paragraphs
- increasing **line spacing** (the spacing between lines in a paragraph)

---

[15] Syntactically incorrect constructions are conventionally indicated by way of an initial asterisk.

- inserting headings and subheadings regularly.

2.3.1 Spacing

While there is a compelling case for different spacings for (a) headings, (b) body text paragraphs, (c) **bulleted** or **numbered list** paragraphs, and (d) caption paragraphs under tables or figures, it is important that the vertical spacing and line spacing of each type of paragraph be consistent.

Document appearance is enhanced if the vertical spacing before each type of paragraph varies as follows:

- Level 1 (top-level) headings should ideally each start on a new page.
- Level 2 headings should have the maximum vertical spacing, with lower-level headings having successively less vertical spacing.
- Body text paragraphs should have no more vertical spacing than the lowest-level headings.
- **Bulleted** and **numbered list** paragraphs may have a smaller vertical spacing than body text paragraphs.

2.3.2 Justification

While **justified** paragraphs[16] are appropriate in books and periodicals, left-aligned text is better in technical and business documents. This is because the space between words varies in justified paragraphs. If your style guide specifies justified paragraphs:

- avoid long white spaces within text by left aligning rather than justifying (a) **bulleted** and **numbered list** paragraphs, and (b) cells in tables

---

[16] A justified paragraph is one with a flush right margin.

- consider rewording any sentence that has long white spaces due to movement of a long word at the end of a line to the start of the next line.

2.3.3   Indents

The left indent of each type of paragraph should vary as follows:

- Level 1 (top-level) headings should have the minimum indent, typically 0" (0 cm).
- Lower-level headings may either have the minimum indent or successively greater indents.
- Body text paragraphs should have at least the maximum indent.
- It is standard practice to give **bulleted** and **numbered list** paragraphs a greater indent than body text paragraphs.

2.3.4   Fonts

Serif fonts are more readable than sans serif fonts for body text. Use a sans serif font for headings and consider using one additional font for any special text, such as examples of computer code. Use only fonts that are commonly available on all operating systems, otherwise some readers' computers may substitute inappropriate fonts.

Use at least 10 point for body text and at least 12 point for headings. Higher-level headings may use larger fonts than lower-level headings, but never smaller fonts. If each level is given a different font size, make sure that the variation between consecutive levels is consistent (for example, decrease by two points for each level).

2.3.5   Consistency

All paragraphs of each type should have the same spacing, justification, left indent, and fonts.

The best way to achieve this is to create a separate style in your word processor for each paragraph type, with appropriate values for (a) before and after vertical spacing, (b) line spacing, (c) justification, (d) left indent, (e) font, and (f) whether each paragraph of that type starts on a new page.

Do not introduce empty paragraphs by pressing the Enter key more than once in succession, as this creates inconsistent vertical spacing.

2.3.6 Tables

Distinguish headings from other content by (a) using bold text for headings, and (b) separating the heading row from the next row by a heavier (or double) line. Set the option "Repeat as header row at the top of each page" ON for the heading row. Set the option "Allow row to break across pages" OFF for all rows. Ensure that all table cells are top aligned rather than center or bottom aligned (although the header row can be bottom aligned).

Text in tables can be (a) in a sans serif font, and (b) smaller than body text.

The tables in this book follow these conventions.

2.3.7 Emphasis

If a word or phrase needs emphasis, render it in bold and/or italic, but not underlining, as that is used for hyperlinks. Do not use color, in case the document is printed in black and white.

Chapter 3. Choice of wording

Arguably the single greatest contribution to the readability of a document is the writer's choice of wording. This chapter focuses on:

- words and phrases that technical writers should use
- wording to clearly distinguish facts, opinions, and assumptions
- wording to indicate obligation, capability, or prohibition
- words and phrases to avoid.

3.1 The language of the organization

Each organization has its own vocabulary, most of which is common across the industry in which it operates, although organizations may create their own additional terms for key concepts. Some organizations document that vocabulary in a **business glossary**, which lists and defines the terms used in discourse (a) internally within the organization, and (b) externally between the organization and its customers, suppliers, and partners.

Most glossaries include only **noun phrases**[17]; some may also standardize **verb phrases**[18]. For example, a university might use standard verb phrases as in "a person applies for a course", "the institution offers a person a place", "a person accepts, rejects or defers an offer", and "a person enrolls in a course". If the glossary does not include verb phrases, it may be possible to infer them from any

---

[17] Defined in Section 9.9.1.
[18] Defined in Sections 9.9.2 and 9.9.3.

nominalizations (nouns formed from verbs or adjectives) in the glossary, in this case "application", "offer", "acceptance", "rejection", "deferral", and "enrollment".[19]

If there is no glossary, the writer of any technical document must consult with relevant business stakeholders to verify the terms used, then include those terms and their definitions in the document. If more than one document is to be produced and there is no glossary, the best approach is to produce an additional document with all terms and their definitions and refer to it in each other document produced. This additional document can then, if endorsed by the organization, become the initial version of that organization's business glossary. Section 5.6.1 discusses business glossaries and the process of creating them.

3.2 Technical terms

As well as the organization's own terminology, any technology or method used by an organization inevitably comes with its own technical terms. These provide a concise means of referring to concepts that would otherwise require long **noun phrases**. For example, "Each entity class is represented by a rectangle in the Entity-Relationship Diagram." is more concise than !"Each data model artifact that represents a class of people, places, things, or other concepts of interest to an enterprise is represented by a rectangle in the diagram representing the organization's business concepts and the relationships between them."[20]

Each technical term used should have a single meaning within the technical or business community. Unfortunately, there are terms in the IT industry that have been **overloaded**: used carelessly, so that they have accrued multiple meanings over time. One notorious example is "**conceptual data model**", for which there are

---

[19] In UK usage, "enrolls" and "enrollment" are spelled "enrols" and "enrolment" respectively.
[20] Any text that is grammatical but not recommended is preceded by an exclamation mark.

multiple conflicting definitions in IT literature. This, and other terms similarly abused, should be avoided. Overloading may also occur when a term with only one meaning is used carelessly, as discussed in Section 7.9.

IT communities regularly create new terms. Many of these are merely synonyms of more familiar terms, which should be used rather than the new terms[21] if all readers are to understand what has been written.

However, if a new term provides a concise label for a complex concept, its use may help reduce sentence length. For example, both "end-user perspective" and "look and feel" mean "the appearance and behavior of a product from the point of view of those who will use it", the latter being less formal.

It is important to use the correct term for each technical concept. For example:

- **Entity-relationship models** consist of "entity classes" (or "entities"), which may be "subtypes" or "supertypes" of other entities. Each entity has "attributes" and "relationships".
- **Object class models** consist of "object classes", which may be "subclasses" or "superclasses" of other object classes. Each object class has "attributes" and "associations".
- **Relational databases** and **object-relational databases** contain "tables" with "rows" and "columns" (not "records" and "attributes"). One or more columns in each table form that table's "primary key". Columns containing references to a primary key (in the same or a different table) form "foreign keys".
- Each variety of **post-relational database** uses a particular terminology, which the writer should follow.

---

[21] See Section 3.9.3.

- Files outside a database are usually known as **"flat files"**, containing **"records"**, which in turn contain **"fields"**.
- **User interfaces** contain a wide variety of components, listed in Section 5.5.2.4.
- In an **operating system** such as Windows, a **"document"** is any file other than a multimedia file (**"image"**, **"video recording"**, or **"sound recording"**). However, the term **"document"** often means only a word processor document, as distinct from a spreadsheet, slide presentation, or other software output. Where there is a risk of confusion, use the term **"word processor document"**.
- Use the right verb: rather than **"model the data vault Customer Hub"**, write **"model Customer data"** or **"design the data vault Customer Hub"**.

Since there is no guarantee that all potential readers will already be familiar with the technical terms in a document, they should all be defined within that document. Moreover, readers must be able to easily locate each definition. Section 4.2 discusses how to manage definitions in a document.

3.3 Names

Refer to persons, organizational positions, organization units, businesses and other organizations, products, nations, and federations by their correct names.

Check the name and preferred title (such as **"Ms"** or **"Dr"**) of any person referred to in a document. Typically, one only needs to use each person's full name on the first occasion, then just the title and surname on subsequent occasions. However, if the document refers to more than one person with the same surname, those persons' full names should be used throughout. The full name consists of the title (optional), first given name, middle initial (in US usage), and surname.

The name of any organization unit or position mentioned, such as **"Operations Department"** or **"Chief Information Officer"**, should also be correctly written: refer to the organization's departmental directory. Only abbreviate these if that is acceptable practice in the organization.

Depending on the situation, refer to a business or other organization by its company name, business name, or one of its registered trading names.

Always correctly identify products such as software, with the version number where necessary, as in "Windows 10" or "SQL Server 2022".

Depending on the situation, refer to a nation by either its official name or the name by which it is commonly known, thus "The United States of America" or "The United States"[22]; "The Democratic People's Republic of Korea" or "North Korea". If referring to a nation more than once, it is usually sufficient to use the official name on only the first occasion.

If a business, other organization, nation, or federation has well-known initials (such as "IBM", "CIA", "the US", or "the EU"), those initials may be used. There are other, less well-known initials, such as "the UAE". If there are multiple references to such a nation or federation, include the full name with the first use of the initials, as in "the United Arab Emirates (UAE)", after which use just the initials.

The name "Great Britain" refers to a geographic entity excluding Northern Ireland, so use "The United Kingdom" or "the UK" when referring to the entire nation.

When referring to the government of a nation, it may be acceptable to use the name of the capital as an alias, as when using "Washington" to refer to the US government.

---

[22] Although "America" is often used to refer to the United States, it is inappropriate in formal writing, since "America" can also refer to all of North and South America.

Each placename should be followed by either (a) the state, province, or territory name or abbreviation as in "London, Ontario", "Flagstaff, AZ", or (b) the country name, as in "Berlin, Germany".

3.4 Adjectives

Adjectives qualify nouns, either (a) by describing an attribute of what the noun refers to (as in "this value is incorrect"), or (b) by limiting the noun to referring only to instances with that attribute (as in "all incorrect values will be reviewed").

Business glossaries rarely (if ever) list adjectives, so choose them carefully:

- Only include an adjective if it adds essential meaning, such as:
    - one that describes a relevant and provable attribute of the person(s) or thing(s) to which a **noun phrase** refers, such as "up-to-date" in "this data is up-to-date"
    - one that qualifies a noun phrase so that it refers only to person(s) or thing(s) with that attribute, such as "updated" in "only updated data is backed up".
- Verb **participles** such as "updated", "written", or "governing" act as adjectives.
- Be sure of the meaning of each adjective you use. For example:
    - Refer to a phenomenon or quantity as "significant" only if it is important or large enough to have an impact.
    - Refer to a technology as "sophisticated" only if it is complicated (in which case "complex", "elaborate", or "intricate" may be suitable alternatives).

3.5 Adverbs

Adverbs (and **adverb phrases**) perform various functions:

- as **linking phrases**, discussed in Section 2.2.3.2

- to provide temporal or spatial information about an event described in a sentence:
    - when it occurs: for example, "eventually", "immediately", "later", "now", "previously", "recently", "soon", "still", "subsequently", "yet"
    - its frequency: for example, "daily", "weekly", "monthly", "yearly", "always", "frequently", "never", "rarely", "sometimes", "usually"
    - where it occurs: for example, "everywhere", "here", "nowhere"
    - its direction of movement (if any): for example, "forward", "backward", "upward", "downward"
- to specify the degree to which something occurs: for example, "barely", "highly", "somewhat", "too", "totally", "less", "least", "more", "most"
- to specify how something occurs: for example, "cautiously", "deliberately", "precisely".

Be aware that **"twice daily"** and **"twice yearly"** do not have the same meanings as **"12-hourly"** and **"six-monthly"** respectively.

Adverbs, like adjectives, rarely appear in business glossaries, so choose them carefully:

- Only include an adverb if it adds essential meaning.
- Avoid vague adverbs such as **"quite"**, **"rather"**, **"really"**, and **"very"**.
- Avoid commonly misused adverbs such as **"basically"**, **"hopefully"**, **"literally"**, and **"thankfully"**.

3.6 Pronouns and determiners

Use a **pronoun**[23] only if it is clear what it refers to. For example, in !"if a row in table NEW_COURSE duplicates a row in table COURSE, it should be deleted"[24], it is not clear which table the row should be deleted from. However, the impersonal pronouns "it" (as in "it is clear") and "one" (as in "one can infer") do not need to refer to anything previously mentioned.

Similarly, use a **demonstrative determiner** ("this", "that", "these", or "those") only if it is clear what it refers to. For example, in "This issue must be resolved." there must be something (and only one thing) in the previous sentence to which "this issue" can refer.

The pronouns "I", "me", and "mine", and the **possessive determiners** "my" and "our", should not appear in technical documents, although they are appropriate in interoffice communications. If a technical document written by a single writer contains any of that author's opinions or references to their experience, the author may refer to his or herself as "the author". In a document produced by multiple writers, the writers may refer to themselves as "we" or "the authors". In a document produced by an organization providing technical services, the writer(s) may refer to that organization by its business name initially, then as "we".

---

[23] Defined in Section 9.4.

[24] Any text that is grammatical but not recommended is preceded by an exclamation mark.

The pronouns "you" and "yours" and the possessive determiner "your" should not be used in technical documents other than interoffice communications and user manuals.[25]

Most communities consider it unacceptable to use "he", "him", "his", and "himself" throughout a document to refer to people irrespective of gender. There are various alternatives:

- "he or she", "him or her", "his or her", "his or hers", "himself or herself"
- "he/she", "him/her", "his/her", "his/hers" , "himself/herself"
- "they", "them", "their", "theirs", "themselves", even when referring to single individuals
- alternating "he", "him", "his", and "himself" with "she", "her", "hers", and "herself".

This is not just political correctness. It is also necessary to use one of the first three alternatives when:

- a person's gender is unknown, as in "The previous manager did not leave their forwarding address." or
- a statement using a singular noun may refer to a person of either gender, as in "Each team member must acquaint themselves with the standard."

In an organization in which staff may specify their preferred pronouns, documents produced for that organization should respect those preferences.

3.7 Facts, opinions, and assumptions

It is important to clearly distinguish facts, opinions, and assumptions.

---

[25] Although "we", "our", "ours", "you", "your", and "yours" are now common in contracts between retail providers and the public, they have no place in business-to-business contracts.

A statement of fact may be self-evident (such as "an integer column can store only whole numbers"), or common knowledge among readers (such as "this database holds all information on our customers"). Readers may not accept other statements of fact unless they can see proof. While proof might appear in the document, it is often better to refer to an authoritative book or article which supports the statement. Section 4.9 discusses such references.

A statement of opinion may represent an opinion of the writer(s) or an opinion of a recognized authority in the relevant field. If it represents an opinion of the writer(s), precede it with a linking clause such as "It is our understanding that" or "Our experience suggests that" (or, if there is only one writer, "It is the author's understanding that" or "The author's experience suggests that"). If it represents an opinion of a recognized authority, a useful linking phrase is "According to <citation>," where "<citation>" is as described in Section 4.9. When the opinion is based on customary practice (and there is evidence that such practice is appropriate), the statement should start with a phrase such as "It is customary practice to". Similarly, when multiple approaches to a particular problem are in common use, the phrases "There is a case for" and "One school of thought is that" may be used. However, if you do, make sure you are not straying into "weasel word" territory[26].

A problem may occur when products of a particular technology or software type appear to all exhibit a particular feature, but there are too many products of that type to verify, within the time available, whether that feature is indeed common to all. In this case, a statement like "most (if not all) database products support foreign keys" avoids contradiction of the statement by later discovery of a counterexample. Similarly, one can use a statement like "few (if any) products

---

[26] See Section 3.9.6.

exhibit this feature" when none of the products reviewed exhibit the feature but there may be others that do.

The writer should list any assumptions that underpin any statement or argument made in a document; the list of assumptions should be in a separate section in that document, with the heading "Assumptions".

3.8 Obligation, capability, prohibition

The **modals** "can", "could", "may", "might", "must", "shall", "should", and "will"[27] are useful in expressing obligations (such as mandatory requirements), capabilities, and prohibitions.

Organizations differ in their preferred terms:

- NASA mandates "shall" to state requirements, but "will" to state purpose, as in "The supplied system will be used to support all billing operations. It shall support 1,000 simultaneous users."

- Most other US government organizations specify "must" rather than "shall" for mandatory requirements or legal obligations, in accordance with the Plain Writing Act of 2010.

- The International Organization for Standardization (ISO) specifies:
    - "shall" for mandatory requirements
    - "should" for desirable features
    - "must" for constraints or obligations defined outside the document in question
    - "can" (not "could") to express capability
    - "may" (not "might") to express permission.

---

[27] The other modal is "would" but has no role in such expressions.

Express prohibitions using "must not" rather than "may not": the sentence !"These columns may not be null." might mean (a) they must not be null, or (b) there is no guarantee that they are null.

3.9   Words and phrases to avoid

3.9.1   Foreign words and phrases

Although some Latin and French words and phrases have entered mainstream English, it is better to avoid those that readers may not understand or may misinterpret.

Some Latin and French words and phrases (a) have become entrenched in English, (b) have no concise English equivalent, and (c) most readers would understand. These include "addendum", "ad hoc", "agenda", "etc.", "memorandum", "per se", "verbatim", "via", "vice versa", "fait accompli", "laissez-faire", and "alias" (as a **noun** meaning "alternative name" or a **preposition** meaning "also known as"). Most readers would also understand the Latin abbreviations "a.m." and "p.m.".

Others have concise English equivalents, which one should use instead. These include "as per" (consistent with, according to, in accordance with), "bona fide" (genuine), "circa" (about), "de facto" (acting), "gratis" (free), "in situ" (in place), "modus operandi" (normal practice), "per annum" (yearly), "per diem" (daily), "pro rata" (in proportion), "re" (about), "status quo" (the existing situation), "à propos" (with respect to), "au fait" (familiar), and "carte blanche" (complete freedom).

The phrase "pro forma" is often used in business documents to mean "template". However, it has a specific legal meaning, and should therefore be avoided.

The abbreviations "e.g." and "i.e." are often confused with each other, so it is better to replace "e.g." by "for example" or "such as" and "i.e." by "that is".

While most readers understand "etc.", the style guide in force may suggest it be replaced by "and so on".

The Latin word "per" on its own (not following "as") has multiple meanings, including "according to", "by means of", "in keeping with", and "for each". It should only be used in expressions such as "per year", "per month", "per week", "per day", "per hour", and "per item", in all of which it means "for each".

Style guides vary as to whether foreign words and phrases should be in italics.

3.9.2 Archaic language

Some once-common words and phrases are no longer so common, so may not be understood by readers. Table 2 lists some examples, along with more understandable alternatives.

Archaic word or phrase	Alternative
aforementioned or aforesaid	stated previously
albeit	although or but
amongst	among
henceforth	from now on or from here on
hereby	by this means
herein	in this document
hereinafter	later in this document
hereto	to this document
heretofore	previously
herewith	enclosed or attached
inasmuch as or insofar as	since
nevertheless or nonetheless	all the same or even so
notwithstanding	although
thence	from there
thereafter	after that
thereby or thereupon	therefore or thus
thereto	to that
therewith	with that
whereupon	at which point
wherewithal	means or resources

Table 2: Archaic language

3.9.3 Buzzwords

The IT and management communities regularly coin (or repurpose) words and phrases in place of better-known alternatives, some with no obvious justification. Table 3 and Table 4 list some common examples.

Jargon term	Alternative(s)	Jargon term	Alternative(s)
bandwidth	time, resources	leveraging	capitalizing
ecosystem	organization, industry	onboarding	induction
impact	affect, effect	unpack	analyze
learnings	lessons	upskill	train, educate

Table 3: Buzzwords

Jargon term	Alternative(s)	Jargon term	Alternative(s)
360 degree	comprehensive	leading edge	innovative
all singing all dancing	with a full suite of features	learning curve	learning period
at the end of the day	in the end, ultimately	low hanging fruit	easily achieved
bells and whistles	features, useful features	marketing collateral	marketing material
best practice	best method	mission critical	of critical importance
blue sky thinking	creative problem-solving	move the goalposts	change the objectives
boil the ocean	be too ambitious	moving forward	in future
circle back	discuss later	on an upward trajectory	increasing
core competency	main area of expertise	on the same page	in agreement
deep dive	thorough investigation	push the envelope	test the limits
drill down	obtain more detail	ramp up	build up
face time	face to face	reach out	communicate
from the get-go	from the start	reinvent the wheel	redo existing work needlessly
gain traction	show real progress	sacred cow[28]	immune from criticism
game changer	significant change	silver bullet	effective solution
heavy lifting	the most difficult tasks	take it offline	discuss it later
kept in the loop	kept informed	think outside the box/square	be creative
key takeaways	important points	win-win	mutual benefit

Table 4: Buzz phrases

---

[28] Another good reason not to use this phrase is that it is offensive to Hindus.

The management and IT communities have also assigned new meanings to some existing terms:

- The **noun phrase** "straw man" is often used in software development circles to mean "prototype created for criticism and testing", although its original meanings were (a) "someone with little integrity or substance", (b) "argument set up to be easily refuted", or (c) "cover for a dubious transaction": "prototype" should be sufficient.
- The **verb** "socialize" (as in "we will then socialize the proposal") now regularly replaces "communicate", which is a clearer and better-understood term.
- The verbs "architect" and "engineer" often replace "design" and "build" respectively, which are less pretentious terms that the reader is more likely to understand.
- Managers often use the verb "address" to mean "discuss" or (occasionally) "analyze", "remedy", or "rectify"; use the verb that accurately describes the activity.

The preposition "around" appears to be replacing "about", "affecting", "to do with", and "associated with". For example:

- !"a stakeholder meeting was held around this issue" rather than "we conducted a stakeholder meeting about this issue"
- !"there are various issues around this functionality" rather than "there are various issues affecting this functionality".

Often "around" follows "conversation", as in !"we had a stakeholder conversation around this issue" rather than "we discussed this issue with stakeholders".

3.9.4   Headline language

While shorter words usually send a clearer message, some short words found in tabloid headlines are inappropriate in technical writing. Use "cancel" rather than "axe"; "reach" or "affect" rather than "hit"; "dispute" or "disagreement" rather than "clash"; and "consider" rather than "mull".

3.9.5 Sales and marketing language

Even if you have consulted marketing material from a technology vendor, you should avoid any words that are either emotional (such as "exciting") or hard to verify or quantify (such as "innovative", "sophisticated", "next generation", or "paradigm shift").

3.9.6 Weasel words

Weasel words are those that create the impression of specific and authoritative meaning but are vague or ambiguous. For example, starting a sentence with "Evidence suggests that" or "Experts agree that" suggests that what follows is an authoritative statement, yet without citing the evidence or identifying even one expert, the entire sentence carries little weight. Similarly, using the **passive voice**, as in "It is said that" raises the question as to who said it (and whether they spoke with any authority).

3.9.7 Words with multiple meanings

Avoid words that have multiple meanings unless the intended meaning is clear from the context. For example:

- The word "argument" means (a) "statement" (of reasons for a particular position or decision), (b) "discussion", (c) "disagreement", (d) "dispute", or (e) "altercation". Instead of "argument", use whichever of these other words most accurately describes what has occurred.
- The word "aggravate", once meaning "exacerbate", now has the meaning "irritate" or "exasperate". Instead of "aggravate", use "exacerbate" if an issue or problem is made worse.

A common source of multiple word meanings is the repurposing of existing words by the IT industry, for example "platform", now also used to mean "set of technologies". If "platform" appears with that meaning in a document produced by an IT project in the rail transport industry, there may be confusion with its rail industry meanings. Another repurposed word is "client" as in "client/server": there may be confusion if this word appears with both its traditional and IT industry meanings.

3.9.8 Ambiguous phrases

Some phrases can be interpreted in more than one way.

3.9.8.1 Parsing ambiguity

An **adjective** before two **nouns** may be ambiguous. For example, !"invalid row deletion" could mean the deletion of invalid rows or the invalid deletion of rows. Whenever you consider using an adjective-noun-noun construction, check it for ambiguity, and rephrase it if ambiguous. In this case, write "the deletion of invalid rows" or "the invalid deletion of rows", whichever is appropriate.

Ambiguity may result from the use of nouns which can qualify other nouns. For example, since "governance" can (a) stand alone as a noun or (b) qualify nouns like "process", "stronger governance and financial processes" could mean "stronger governance processes and stronger financial processes" or "financial processes and stronger governance".

3.9.8.2 Ambiguous modals

A reader might interpret !"A customer may not enter this data." as (a) the customer must not do so, or (b) they might neglect to do so. Always use "must not" to express a prohibition.

3.9.8.3 Ambiguous expressions of time

A reader can only confidently interpret an expression of time such as "today", "tomorrow", "yesterday", "this week", "last month", and "next year" if they know when it was written. Such expressions are acceptable in a dated interoffice communication, but not in a permanent document. This is particularly true of documents that have undergone revisions, as it may not be clear whether such an expression is relative to the original publication date or one of the revision dates.

Always include specific dates (and times if necessary): a complete date if known, a month and year if the day of the month is unknown, or a year alone if the month is unknown. Section 4.5.1 provides a guide to writing dates in a document.

3.9.9 Double negatives

Two negatives in a single clause can be used validly to cancel each other out, as in "this is not uncommon", although the simpler construction (in this case, "this is common") is better. However, it is invalid to use two negatives to intensify the negativity, as in *"there are no empty tables in none of the databases"[29]. To express this in Standard English, use only one negative, as in "there are no empty tables in any of the databases", "there are empty tables in none of the databases", or "none of the databases has empty tables".

---

[29] Syntactically incorrect constructions are conventionally indicated by way of an initial asterisk.

3.9.10 Redundancy

Remove redundant words, such as:

- "close" from "close scrutiny"
- "exact" from "exact same"
- "past" from "past history"

Including both "reason" and "because" is redundant. Rephrase !"the reason for this message is because ..." as "the reason for this message is ..." or "this message is displayed because ...".

3.9.11 Synonyms and contranyms

Using multiple **synonyms** to refer to the same concept may cause confusion. For example, if a document contains both "client" and "customer" with the same meaning, readers may become distracted by the possibility of a difference in meaning. If each term has a different meaning, a document may contain both, but should include definitions of both.

If the organization uses multiple terms with the same meaning, the writer should establish which is the preferred term. If there is one preferred term, use it. If there is no preference, choose one and use only that one.

A **contranym** is a word that has multiple meanings that contradict each other. One should avoid using these, using instead an appropriate synonym that has only one meaning, or a meaning that the reader can easily infer from the context. Examples of contranyms (with their alternative meanings, which should be used instead) are:

- "consult": to "advise" or "seek advice"
- "hold up": to "support" or "impede"
- "oversight": "supervision" or "failure to check"

- "sanction": to "approve" or "boycott"
- "variety": one "type" or "multiple types"
- "with": "alongside" or "against".

3.9.12 Long noun chains

A **noun chain** is a sequence of two or more nouns used to express a single concept, such as "Asset Management System" or "user manual". Chains of two or three nouns like these are easy to understand, but the longer the chain, the less understandable it may be. For example, instead of !"Asset Management System User Manual", it might be better to write "User Manual for the Asset Management System".

3.9.13 Contractions

Contractions are short forms of words or phrases created by omitting internal letters. Avoid them in technical writing other than emails or other informal interoffice communications. The "'s" form used to denote possession is of course acceptable in technical or business writing.

Table 5 lists types of contractions used in English.

Contraction	Long form	Examples
'd	had or would	he'd
'll	will	we'll
'm	am	I'm
n't	not	don't
're	are	we're
's	is or has	she's, it's, who's, how's
's	us	let's
've	have	I've, would've
<noun phrase>'s	is or has	the system's offline

Table 5: Contractions

Chapter 4. Specific content

This chapter covers a variety of content for which there are specific rules:

- **series** (lists): Section 4.1
- definitions: Section 4.2
- quoted material: Section 4.3
- abbreviations: Section 4.4
- various forms of numeric information such as dates and times, monetary amounts, quantities, percentages, measurements, numeric identifiers, and ordinal numbers: Section 4.5
- diagrams: Section 4.6
- navigational aids such as headings, cross-references, and references to other documents or published works: Sections 4.7 to 4.9
- **front matter** (information about a document included at the beginning): Section 4.10.

4.1 Series

A **series** is a list of two or more words, phrases, clauses, or sentences, each denoting one of a set of similar items, such as attributes, steps, or options. A series may be set out in any of the following ways:

- **inline**, as in:
    - "the software is effective, efficient, and inexpensive"
    - "the transaction is then committed or rolled back"
    - "the team have tested all updates, regression tested existing functionality, and installed the new release"
- inline, but with distinguishing letters or numbers, as in "the transaction is then (a) committed, or (b) rolled back" or "the team have 1) tested all updates, 2) regression tested existing functionality, and 3) installed the new release"

- with each item in a separate paragraph starting with:
    - a bullet (a **bulleted list**), like this series
    - a sequence number (a **numbered list**), as in Figure 3.

Address updating should proceed as follows:
1. establish which people currently at the old address are moving to the new address
2. create a new address row and link each person identified in step 1 to that new row
3. delete the old address row if and only if everyone currently at the old address is moving to the new address.

Figure 3: A numbered list

If any items in a series are to be referenced elsewhere, use a numbered list. A numbered list implies either chronological sequence or ranking, so be sure to sequence the items appropriately.

A series can be organized hierarchically. This is most easily done using separate paragraphs, although a hierarchic series of short items can be written in line, as in:

- "This week we can (a) finish testing remaining enhancements and package the new version, or (b) complete the specification of the next version and circulate it to stakeholders."
  (using distinguishing letters for top-level items but omitting any distinguishing letters or numbers for lower-level items), or
- "This form captures the name, birth date, and passport number of each passenger; the date and flight number of each flight; and the number, account name, and expiry date of the credit card used for payment."
  (using semicolons to separate top-level items and commas to separate lower-level items).

If using separate paragraphs, distinguish levels as follows:

- In a **bulleted list**, use a different bullet symbol at each level.
- In a **numbered list**, use a different numbering scheme at each level.

Figure 4 illustrates both techniques.

> Daylight saving is generally only an issue for:
>
> - enterprises with operations in more than one jurisdiction where:
>   - some of those jurisdictions observe daylight saving while others do not (e.g., States in the US and Australia), or
>   - those jurisdictions may change to or from daylight saving on different dates (e.g., States in Australia), or
> - enterprises with overnight processes which may traverse a change to or from daylight saving (e.g., overnight flights or train schedules).
>
> Each business key in each table must be rendered as follows:
>
> 1. Capitalise the first (and only the first) letter of:
>   a. the first word
>   b. each noun and adjective
> 2. Render in all lower case
>   a. each article (a, an, the)
>   b. each conjunction (e.g., and)
>   c. each preposition (e.g., of, for, to).

Figure 4: Hierarchic lists

Other techniques may be employed, such as:

- using numbered top-level paragraphs and bulleted lower-level paragraphs
- using numbered or bulleted top-level paragraphs and listing lower-level items inline.

Section 6.4 covers the rules governing series.

4.2 Definitions

All technical terms used in a document should be defined, in that document or another document available to the reader. The definition for each term may be (a) inline (immediately after the term), (b) in a footnote, (c) in a separate section of the document, or (d) in a separate glossary document or resource.

If definitions are in a separate section of the document, that section should be at the end of the document rather than the start.[30]

An inline definition may appear in the form of (a) a sentence, as in "A mandatory attribute is one for which every instance of the entity class must have a value.", or (b) a parenthetical within a sentence using the term, as in "Each mandatory attribute (one for which every instance of the entity class must have a value) is marked in bold in the diagram."

If the definition is elsewhere in the document, add a cross-reference to the section containing the definition (such as "See Section 9.9") either (a) inline (immediately after the term), or (b) in a footnote. For this reason, any definition should be in the first paragraph in its section. Similarly, if the definition is in a separate glossary document or resource, include an appropriate cross-reference.

For each term not commonly used, include the definition or cross-reference:

- with the first use of the term
- wherever the meaning of a term is critical to the meaning of a sentence.

Some documents, particularly data definition documents, may include technical terms from both IT and the organization's industry. For example, a data definition document for a transportation company needs to define industry-specific terms as well as any IT technical terms. If so, it is better to provide separate glossaries for industry-specific and IT terms. In a data definition document, industry-specific term definitions are typically contained in entity or object class definitions (or table definitions).

---

[30] Except in the case of a contract.

A definition in a glossary should not itself be a complete sentence but should form a complete sentence when prefixed by "A <term> is". For example, the definition of "mandatory attribute" should be "one for which every instance of the entity class must have a value." The term and its definition together form the sentence depicted earlier in this section.

Other quality criteria for definitions are:

- No definition should be misleading, by causing a reader to infer either a broader or narrower meaning of the term than the intended meaning.
- The definition should include at least one of "a", "an", "any", or "one". For example, "the Party who lends money under the terms of a Mortgage" is an acceptable definition of "Mortgagee", but "the Party who lends money under the terms of the Mortgage" is not. This is because a definition should apply to all instances of the term.
- All nouns in a definition should be either in common use or defined elsewhere in the glossary. If defined elsewhere, they should be marked in some way, ideally with a hyperlink for onscreen readers.

4.3 Quoted material

When quoting a speaker or writer:

- enclose the quote in quotation marks
- if, to provide clarity, it is necessary to replace any quoted words with others, simply omit the replaced words and enclose the replacement words in square brackets ("[" and "]")—for example, if the quoted passage reads "they decided to replace the system early the following year", this could be quoted as "[the committee] decided to replace the system early [in 2020]"

- use the ellipsis symbol ("...") in place of each set of consecutive words that are omitted from the quotation without being replaced—for example, if the quoted passage reads "the committee decided, after due deliberation, to replace the system in question, as well as others, early in 2020", this could be quoted as "the committee decided ... to replace the system ... early in 2020".

There are rules governing the use of other punctuation marks before and after quoted text. These vary between style guides and are discussed in Section 6.7.14.

4.4 Abbreviations

An abbreviation is a shortened form of a word or phrase. Abbreviations of single words involve the removal of letters from the middle or the end, as in "Dr" or "Prof" (for "Doctor" and "Professor" respectively). There are abbreviations for many multiple word phrases, each formed from the initial letters of all or most of the words in the phrase, as in "SQL" or "NATO". For this reason, these are known as **initialisms**[31]. Other initialisms, such as "radar"[32], include more than one letter from some words.

4.4.1 Are abbreviations appropriate?

In general, an abbreviation should only be included in a technical document if (a) it is in common use in the organization or community, so that every potential reader will understand its meaning, or (b) it represents a term that occurs throughout the document. Abbreviations that might not be understood by all potential readers should be listed with their meanings at either the start or end

---

[31] Some use the term **acronym** to refer to an initialism that is pronounced as a single word like "NATO", while others use that term to refer to any initialism.

[32] Short for "radio detecting and ranging".

of the document; if they are listed at the end, the document introduction should provide readers with a cross-reference to the location of that list.

The following are acceptable in a technical or business document:

- abbreviations for personal titles (such as "Dr" or "Prof")
- initialisms or codes for states in the country in which the document is published (such as "NY" or "NSW")
- well-known initialisms of:
    - countries, federations, or organizations, such as "US" , "UK", "EU", and "UN"
    - businesses, such as "IBM"
    - organizational roles, such as "CIO"
    - technologies or computer languages, such as "DBMS" or "SQL".

Other abbreviations (such as "Dept" or "Mgr") are not acceptable in a technical document: all words other than personal titles and those forming part of acceptable initialisms or codes should be spelled in full.

If there is a reasonably well-known initialism of a term that is to be used more than once in a particular subsection of a document, it may be introduced the first time the term appears, then used in place of the term in the remainder of the subsection. For example, "The organization is currently running multiple database management systems (DBMSs). The choice of which DBMS to use depends on several criteria. We will advise which DBMS we have selected once we have reviewed how each DBMS meets each criterion."

4.4.2 Capitalization and punctuation conventions

Style guides differ in their conventions for the capitalization and punctuation of abbreviations. If you have established which style guide applies (as described in Section 2.1.3), follow its advice. If not, you should choose a convention and be consistent within a document or set of documents.

An initialism is generally written in all uppercase, unless (like "laser") it has become established as a word in its own right. There are exceptions: in some initialisms that include prepositions, the initial letters of those prepositions may be in lowercase. For example, in initialisms for UK government departments, lowercase "f" represents "for", as in "DfT" ("Department for Transport"). Other abbreviations are in lowercase, except for the first letter, which is in uppercase if the complete word would have an initial uppercase letter in the same position, as in "Dr".

Some style guides specify that there be no periods (full stops) in initialisms or other abbreviations. Others specify no periods in initialisms but periods at the ends of other abbreviations. There are also others that specify periods in all abbreviations. In initialisms with periods, there is one after each letter. Thus "US" and "U.S." are correct, but not "US.". Initialisms do not generally include spaces.

The ampersand symbol ("&") is an abbreviation for "and". It should only be used in technical or business documents in:

- business names, such as "AT&T"
- citations of works by multiple authors, such as "(Simsion & Witt, 2004)".

4.5 Numeric information

Numeric information includes dates, times, quantities, and numeric identifiers. One may represent such information using either numerals (as in "5") or words ("five"). This section sets out the rules for each type of information. There is significant variation between style guides: it is important that a document or set of documents be consistent.

4.5.1 Dates

The following rules govern the representation of dates:

- Use words when a date occurs at the beginning of a sentence, thus "Nineteen forty-eight" or "The year 1948 ...", but not !"1948 ..."[33].
- A year may be represented in words as (for example) "twenty twenty-two", which is acceptable in both US and UK usage. Alternatives are "two thousand and twenty-two" (UK) and "two thousand twenty-two" (US).
- A date may be represented as:
    - just a month and day, but only when the year is clear from the context (for example, followed by "of that year"); in US usage the month name precedes the day number, as in "December 25", whereas in UK usage, the month name follows the day number, as in "25 December"
    - just a month and year, as in "February 2020" (in both US and UK usage)
    - a complete date without a day name, as in "January 1, 2022" (in US usage), "1 January 2022" (in UK usage); do not use all-numeral dates, such as !"7/4/2022" which are ambiguous due to the different conventions
    - a complete date with a day name, either followed by a comma, as in "Monday, December 5, 2022" (in US usage) or not, as in "Monday 5 December 2022" (in UK/Australian usage). Some UK publications include a comma after the day name.
- In US usage, the first nine days of a month are represented using words (as in "the first of each month"), whereas other days use an ordinal (as in "the 20th of each month". In Australian usage, any day of the month may be represented using an ordinal (as in "the 1st"). If an ordinal is used,

---

[33] However, the Associated Press Stylebook allows a numeric year at the start of a sentence.

most (if not all) style guides require the ordinal suffix to be rendered normally (as in the examples here) rather than as a superscript.

- A decade may be represented as a numeral (as in "the '80s") or a word (as in "the eighties"); some guides require the word form.
- In tables, charts, and other graphic content:
    - A month name may be abbreviated to the first three letters, except May to July or March to July in US usage, depending on the style guide, and September, which is abbreviated either to "Sept" or "Sep".
    - Some style guides allow day names other than Tuesday or Thursday to be abbreviated to the first one or three letters (as in "M", "Mon") and Tuesday and Thursday to be abbreviated either to "Tu" and "Th" or "Tues" and "Thurs".
    - Style guides vary as to whether an abbreviated month or day name should be followed by a period (full stop).
- Some style guides specify that "thru" (in US usage), "to" (in UK usage), or "until" (US and UK usage) should be used between dates rather than a dash or hyphen, as in "from Jan until June" or "from 1999 until 2019". In Australia at least, fiscal years[34] are an exception, so one may write "the 2020–21 financial year".
- Use "on" before a complete date or month and day, "in" otherwise, thus "on January 1, 2022" but "in January 2022".

4.5.2   Times of day

The following rules govern the representation of times of day:

- These may be represented using a 12-hour clock, as in "1:30 p.m.", or a 24-hour clock, as in "13:30".

---

[34] Known as financial years in Australia.

- Style guides vary in specifying how to write "a.m." and "p.m.":
    - Some specify lowercase (as in the examples so far), while others specify uppercase or small capitals.
    - Some specify periods (full stops) after each letter, while others specify no periods.
    - Some specify that a full hour in the 12-hour clock may be written with or without the minutes (as in "9:00 am" or "9 am"), while others specify that full hours may only be written without the minutes. However, all 24-hour clock times must include minutes, as in "17:00" rather than !"17".
- Most (if not all) style guides specify:
    - a colon between the hours and minutes, in both the 12-hour and 24-hour clocks, although some UK style guides allow, or even recommend, a period (full stop) as an alternative
    - a **nonbreaking space**[35] between the numerals and "am" or "pm"
    - "noon" or "midnight" rather than !"12 pm" or !"12 am"
    - a leading zero in 24-hour clock times before 10 am, thus "09:30" rather than !"9:30".
- If the time needs to be specified precisely (as in a contract), a time zone code such as "PST", "EDT", "GMT", "BST", "AEST" should be added after the time and a **nonbreaking space**, as in "11:59 AEST".
- Some style guides mandate that "thru" (in US usage), "to" (in UK usage), or "until" (US and UK usage) should be used between times rather than a dash or hyphen, as in "from 9 am until noon".
- Do not add:
    - "in the morning" or "in the afternoon" to a time written (a) with "am" or "pm", or (b) using the 24-hour clock

---

[35] A space character that prevents automatic line breaking, thus keeping the characters before and after it on the same line.

- o "am" or "pm" to a time written using the 24-hour clock.

4.5.3 Monetary amounts

The following rules govern the representation of monetary amounts:

- Use numerals for the amount.
- The currency symbol should precede the amount, without an intervening space, thus "€1,000" rather than !"€ 1,000".
- Commas should be used to separate each set of three digits before the decimal point (if any).
- If the amount is in dollars, there is a risk of confusion as to which currency the amount is specified in, so any such amount should not be written with just "$", but in one of the following ways:
    - o with a letter or letters signifying the country after "$", as in "$US1,000", "$A1,000"[36]
    - o with the appropriate ISO 4217 3-letter code and a **nonbreaking space**[37] before the amount, as in "USD 1,000".

4.5.4 Other quantities

The following rules govern the representation of quantities generally:

- Use words for whole numbers less than 10.
- Use words for a number at the start of a sentence, but where that number requires more than two or three words, use numerals preceded by other words—for example, write "A total of 32,568 rows were deleted." rather than !"Thirty-two thousand five hundred sixty-eight rows were deleted."

---

[36] Some guides allow the letter or letters signifying the country to appear before "$".

[37] A space character that prevents automatic line breaking, thus keeping the characters before and after it on the same line.

- In a single sentence, use either numerals for all numbers or words for all numbers. For example, write "six developers and twelve testers" or "6 developers and 12 testers" rather than !"six developers and 12 testers".

- Where two numbers are adjacent, use words for one and a numeral for the other. For example, write "six 5-column tables" or "6 five-column tables" rather than !"6 5-column tables".

- Write estimated quantities of 1,000 or more with a final word. For example, write "approximately 250 million rows" rather than !"approximately 250,000,000 rows". Some guides allow "k", "m", or "bn" to represent thousands, millions, or billions respectively; if these are used, there is no intervening space, thus "approximately 250m rows"[38].

- Hyphenate numbers between 21 and 100 written as words, as in "sixty-eight", and fractions written as words, as in "three-quarters".

- Use numerals for measurements, ratios, percentages, percentiles, quartiles, and decimal numerals such as "1.25".

- Use commas to separate groups of three digits, as in "32,568".

- For decimal numerals less than 1, include a zero in front of the decimal point, as in "0.75".

- Use an **en dash** or the word "to" rather than a hyphen between the bounds of a range, as in "25–30" or "25 to 30" rather than !"25-30".

Some style guides require the use of words for numbers that can be expressed in only one or two words (as in "one hundred", "ninety-nine"), while others require the use of words only for numbers that can be expressed in one word (as in "ten", "eleven", "thirty").

---

[38] Some guides specify "M" for "million" rather than "m".

4.5.5 Percentages

Style guides vary in specifying how to write percentages:

- Some require that percentages be written in words rather than numerals.
- Some require "per cent" rather than "percent", while others require "percent" rather than "per cent".
- The consensus is that when using numerals there should be no space between the numeral and the "%" symbol.

4.5.6 Measurement units

Unless written in full, measurement units should only be represented using standard abbreviations or symbols. To avoid misinterpretation, a temperature should always be expressed using either "°F" or "°C", not "°" alone.

4.5.6.1 US units

Table 6 lists the US measurement units most likely to appear in a technical document, with their standard abbreviations and symbols (if any). There should be a **nonbreaking space**[39] before any abbreviation, but not before the symbols for feet or inches.

---

[39] A space character that prevents automatic line breaking, thus keeping the characters before and after it on the same line.

Unit	Abbreviation/symbol	Unit	Abbreviation
mile	mi	acre	acre
yard	yd	gallon	gal
foot	ft, '	nautical mile	NM, nmi
inch	in, "	ton	ton
square mile	sq mi, mi²	hundredweight	cwt
square foot	sq ft, ft²	pound	lb
square inch	sq in, in²	ounce	oz
cubic yard	cu yd, yd³	degree Fahrenheit	°F
cubic foot	cu ft, ft³	horsepower	hp
cubic inch	cu in, in³	pound per square inch	psi
miles per hour	mph	miles per gallon	mpg

Table 6: US measurement units

4.5.6.2 International units

Table 7 lists the international ("SI") measurement units most likely to appear in a technical document, with their standard abbreviations. Where a multiplier appears, it precedes the unit symbol without any intervening space, as in "ha", "kPa", "kW", and "MJ". The consensus is that there should be a **nonbreaking space** between the numeral and the abbreviation, although some publications omit such spaces.

Note that multiplier symbols have different meanings when used with bytes and with other units.

Unit	Abbreviation	Multiplier	Abbreviation	Factor	Byte Factor
metre	m	exa	E	10^{18}	$1{,}024^6$
gram	g	peta	P	10^{15}	$1{,}024^5$
square metre	m²	tera	T	10^{12}	$1{,}024^4$
hectare	ha	giga	G	10^9	$1{,}024^3$
litre	L	mega	M	10^6	$1{,}024^2$
kilopascal	kPa	kilo	k	10^3	1,024
kilowatt	kW	hecto	h	10^2	N/A
megajoule	MJ	centi	c	10^{-2}	N/A
kilowatt-hour	kW·h	milli	m	10^{-3}	N/A
ampere	A	micro	μ	10^{-6}	N/A
volt	V	nano	n	10^{-9}	N/A
degree Celsius	°C	pico	p	10^{-12}	N/A
byte	B	femto	f	10^{-15}	N/A
megabyte/second	MB/s				
kilometre/hour	km/h				
litre/100 km	L/100 km				

Table 7: International measurement units

4.5.7 Numeric identifiers

Write numeric identifiers (such as street numbers, postal codes, and chapter, page, and section numbers) using numerals, as in "10 Downing St", "Route 66", "Section 1.2".

4.5.8 Ordinal numbers

Although one may represent an item's position in a sequence by a **noun phrase** such as "the third step", it is preferable to use a numeral after a label, such as "Step 3", "Level 1", "Table 2", or "Section 3.4".

Always capitalize the label (such as "Step", "Level", "Table", or "Section") unless it applies to one or more page or paragraph numbers, for which the norm is a lowercase abbreviation, such as "p. 23", "pp. 23–25", "para. 1", "paras. 1–3".

Use words for ordinals from "first" to "nineth". Numerals may be used for higher ordinals such as "23rd". Style guides vary as to whether the suffix after the numeral should be superscripted (as in "23rd") or not.

4.6 Diagrams

Most diagrams consist of shapes joined by lines. Diagrams should adhere to the following principles if readers are to easily understand them:

- All shapes representing the same type of concept should be the same; not only the same shape (rectangle, diamond, circle) but with the same corners (square or round), **line style** (solid, dashed, or dotted), and **line weight** (thickness).
- If two types of concepts represented in the diagram are significantly different, represent them using different shapes or by shapes with different corners, line styles, or line weights.
- Shapes that are imperfectly aligned (horizontally or vertically) should be aligned using the appropriate diagramming software function. Failure to do this makes the diagram look untidy, which would detract from its use as an information resource.
- All lines representing the same type of relationship should be the same:
    - the same line style (solid, dashed, or dotted) and line weight
    - the same **ornaments** (such as arrowheads, "crows' feet", crossbars, or circles) at the ends or middle of each line.
- If two types of relationships represented in the diagram are significantly different, represent them using different line styles, line weights, or ornaments.
- If possible, avoid introducing more than one bend to any line.

- If possible, lines should not cross each other. If the topology of the diagram requires any crossings, ensure that:
    - the number of crossings is kept to a minimum
    - when any two lines cross, there is a gap or loop in one of them, as depicted in the first two diagrams in Figure 5.

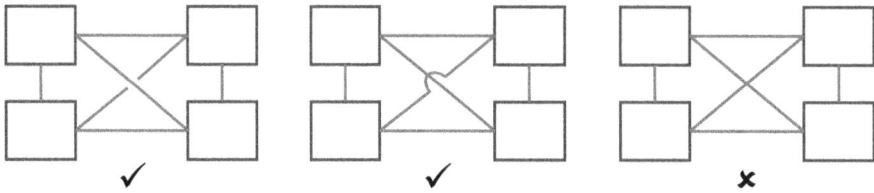

Figure 5: Crossing lines

Figure 6 illustrates some of these principles. Each shape represents an entity class, each dashed line represents a relationship between two independent entity classes, and each solid line represents a relationship between an independent entity class and an entity class that is dependent on it. Each line has the same ornaments except the line between the shapes representing Scheduled Flight and Day of Operation; a Scheduled Flight must have at least one Day of Operation, whereas it may have no Meal Service and there may be Ports without any Scheduled Flights.

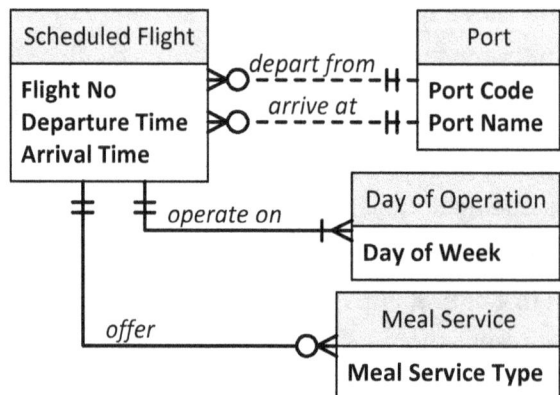

Figure 6: Example of data model diagram

4.7 Headings

Each section and subsection should have a heading: a phrase which summarizes the content of the (sub)section and any lower-level subsections within. The phrase does not have to be a complete sentence: most headings consist of one or more **noun phrases**[40].

Each heading should be numbered, to provide for easy navigation of cross-references between sections. The headings before each top-level section should be numbered in sequence. Each heading before a subsection should be given a number consisting of the number of the parent section, a decimal point, and a subsection number in sequence, as in this book. Word processing software provides automatic numbering of headings.

A heading should not be just a list of topics—such as "Business keys, primary keys, **and surrogate keys**"—unless there is no generic term that encompasses those topics, such as (in this case) "**Database keys**". Such a heading would need to be changed if an additional subsection were added dealing with, say, foreign keys; the writer may forget to do so.

Do not include a period, colon, or any other punctuation mark at the end of a heading.

4.8 Cross-references

When it is necessary to refer to material elsewhere in a document, write "Section" followed by the number of the (sub)section that includes the referenced material.

---

[40] Defined in Section 9.9.1.

Do not type the number as it may change if new material is added or if the document is reorganized. Instead, use the appropriate word processor function to insert a soft cross-reference, and update it before publication. Moreover, onscreen readers of the document can use the resulting soft cross-reference as a hyperlink to enable quick navigation to the referenced section.

4.9 References to other documents or published works

Each reference to another document or published work should use an **in-text citation** at the relevant point in the text. To avoid interrupting the narrative flow, such citations are usually abbreviated rather than including the full details of the referenced work.

If a document refers to other documents produced for the same organization, a common technique is to list all referenced documents in the **front matter**[41] of the referencing document, each with an identifying number. Each citation can then use that identifying number (typically in square brackets) rather than the name of the referenced document.

If a document refers to published books or articles, it should include a bibliography at the end. The format of each entry in the bibliography depends on the nature of the work:

- For a book, the entry lists each author's surname and initials, the publication year, the title and any subtitle, and the publisher, as in
  "Witt, G. C. (2021). *Data Modeling for Quality: Delivering benefits through attention to detail*. Technics Publications." or
  "Date, C. J., Darwen, H., & Lorentzos, N. A. (2003). *Temporal Data and the Relational Model*. Morgan Kaufman."

---

[41] See next section.

If there are multiple entries for the same author(s) in the same year, a common convention is to append a different lowercase letter to the year number in each entry.

- For a work published by an organization, the organization's name replaces the authors' surnames and initials.
- For a chapter in an edited collection of works by different authors, the entry lists each author's surname and initials, the publication year, the title and any subtitle of the chapter, the editor's surname and initials, the title and any subtitle of the book, and the publisher, as in "Witt, G. C. (2008). Logical Database Design. In Teorey, T. J., Lightstone, S., Inmon, W. H., & Buston, S. (Ed.), *Database Design: Know It All*. Morgan Kaufman."
- For a journal article, the entry lists each author's surname and initials, the publication year, the title and any subtitle of the article, the title of the journal, and the volume and issue numbers in which the article was published, as in "Witt, G. C. (1998). The Role of Metadata in Data Quality. *Journal of Data Warehousing*, vol. 3 no. 4." For an article published online, a **digital online identifier** (a persistent link to the content, formatted as a URL) should be added.
- The page number(s), edition number, and place of publication may be added if likely to be useful to the reader.

There are two forms of in-text citation:

- a reference to the work, as in "(Witt, 2021) includes such a technique."
- a reference to the author, as in "This is the technique described by Witt (2021)".

The Chicago Manual of Style allows for an alternative referencing technique using footnotes. Each footnote contains either a complete bibliography entry (as described above) or an abbreviated entry consisting of the author's family name, the book title (without subtitle), and the page number(s).

There are various detail differences between style guides which are outside the scope of this book. The above is only a summary.

4.10 Front matter

The **front matter** of a document provides information about the document. Each organization has its own criteria for inclusion of information in the front matter. Typically, it includes:

- a title page, with the document title, the project or program for which it has been produced, and the organization logo; other information may include the writer's name, the publication date, and the version number
- metadata, including:
    - the document's identifier in the organization's Document Management System
    - a list of published versions, each with version number, publication date, writers, and a brief statement of the changes included
    - the names of the project sponsor and any other key stakeholders
    - the names of the writer(s) and all reviewers
    - a table with spaces for approval signatures and dates
    - a list of known issues
    - guidelines for use
    - disclaimers
- a table of contents
- a table of figures if required.

Chapter 5. Typical documents

This chapter discusses typical documents that a technical writer or other IT professional might produce or review, and guidelines for doing so.

5.1 Document lifecycles

Different document types have different lifespans: some only last for the duration of a project or pre-project negotiations, while others last for as long as a system is in use or the organization continues to operate. The management of versions also varies by document type: some undergo multiple revisions both before and after publication, others only before publication, while others usually have only one version. Table 8 summarizes this variation.

Document type	Lifespan	Versions
Request for Tenders	only until Contract	only before publication
Tender	until project completion	only before publication
Contract	ongoing	only before publication
Pre-project document	until project completion	only before publication
Product review/recommendation	ongoing	only before publication
Requirements Specification	until project completion	ongoing
Software specification	until software retired	ongoing
Change Request	until request met	one
Release Notice	ongoing	one
Progress Report	until project completion	one
Business Glossary	ongoing	ongoing
Technical standards	ongoing	ongoing
User Manual	until software retired	ongoing
Standard Operating Procedures	ongoing	ongoing
Office communications	various	one

Table 8: Document lifecycles

5.2 Inter-organization documents

These are documents produced by one organization and communicated to one or more other organizations.

5.2.1 Requests for Tenders

A Request for Tenders is a formal document (or set of documents) published to potential suppliers by an organization that wishes to acquire goods and/or services. The content of a Request for Tenders must be clear and unambiguous, and must accurately reflect the organization's requirements.

A Request for Tenders is typically produced by a multidisciplinary team. For example, if the Request for Tenders is for the supply of IT software and/or services, both business and technical staff should be involved. There is also generally a need for legal team input. Use of a collaboration tool to manage different document sections and versions produces a better result for less overall effort.

Any technical content should be written by one or more suitably qualified staff and reviewed by other similarly qualified staff, to ensure that all requirements are clearly, unambiguously, and accurately stated.

5.2.2 Tenders

A Tender is a document submitted in response to a Request for Tenders, offering to supply the goods and/or services itemized in that Request for Tenders.

As with a Request for Tenders, a Tender must be written by one or more suitably qualified staff, both technical and legal, and reviewed by other similarly qualified staff. This is to ensure that all statements made about any software or services clearly, unambiguously, and accurately represent what is feasible given the resources and time specified for delivery.

5.2.3 Contracts

A Contract is a document drawn up between a supplier of goods and/or services and the organization purchasing those goods and/or services. While legal rather than technical experts will draft the Contract itself, schedules (appendices) containing technical details are typically attached to a Contract.

As with a Request for Tenders or Tender, such technical detail must be written by one or more suitably qualified staff and reviewed by other similarly qualified staff, to ensure that all technical detail clearly, unambiguously, and accurately represents what is to be delivered.

5.3 Pre-project documents

Before an IT project gets under way, pre-project documents such as Project Proposals and Business Cases are typically produced.

These should state clearly (a) what is proposed; (b) what benefits the proposed technology will confer on the organization; and (c) realistic estimates of the resources, time, and cost of undertaking the project. Although the technical content of such a document is usually high-level rather than detailed, it is important that one or more IT professionals contribute that technical content, to ensure that the proposal is technically feasible and the estimates realistic.

If the organization's decision makers are unsure of how to meet a requirement or set of requirements or are aware that there are multiple ways of doing so, they may commission a product review or recommendations document, either internally or from a consulting firm.

5.4 Product reviews and recommendations

These are produced when there are multiple ways of meeting a requirement or set of requirements. This may mean anything from employing alternative technologies to acquiring and rolling out alternative software products. Irrespective of the types of options being considered, there is a standard process to be followed:

1. Establish the relevant stakeholders from whom to elicit requirements.
2. Interview those stakeholders individually and in workshops to elicit requirements.
3. Document the requirements, publish to stakeholders for review, update the requirements to reflect reviewer comments, and republish (repeat as necessary).
4. Identify those technologies or software products that may support the documented requirements (individually or jointly).
5. Review online documentation about each technology and software product, to verify how well it might support the documented requirements.
6. Propose a shortlist of technologies and/or software products to be investigated in detail and obtain agreement from stakeholders to proceed with that shortlist.
7. Document a set of tests to be conducted on each shortlisted technology or software product, publish this to stakeholders for review, update the test set to reflect reviewer comments, and republish (repeat as necessary).
8. Download a trial version of each shortlisted technology or software product.
9. Conduct the documented tests and record the results. The result of a particular product against a particular test will be one of (a) fully exhibits required functionality, (b) partially exhibits required functionality, or (c) does not exhibit required functionality.

A product review document should include (a) all requirements, (b) each tested product, (c) the results of each test against each product, (d) nonfunctional features of each product, such as pricing, available support levels, and supplier profile, (e) significant differentiators between products' fit to requirements. A Recommendations document should include all these, plus (f) recommendations of which product(s) to purchase.

5.5 IT project documents

5.5.1 Requirements specifications

A Requirements Specification documents an organization's requirements for technology to support one or more business processes. For it to be effective, each requirement must be:

- documented in business language
- individually identified, so that it can be cross-referenced in other documentation
- **atomic**, rather than combining multiple requirements—for example, rather than "123. The system must allow each track to be marked as unidirectional or bidirectional with different speed limits in different directions on bidirectional tracks." these two requirements should be written as:
    - "123. The system must allow each track to be marked as unidirectional or bidirectional.
    - 124. The system must allow for different speed limits in different directions on bidirectional tracks."

The writer of a Requirements Specification must take care to avoid:

- **synonyms**: different terms with the same meaning, such as "Customer" and "Client", or "Train" and "Consist"
- **homonyms**: multiple meanings of a single term, such as "Account", "Line", "Train", or "Service".

If a Requirements Specification contains synonyms, there is the possibility that two different requirements, one using one term and one using another, turn out to be alternative statements of the same requirement. Alternatively, if the two requirements conflict, readers must try to establish which one is correct.

If a Requirements Specification contains homonyms, it may not be clear which meaning applies each time the term appears. The writer should be alert to terms which might have multiple meanings, clarify with business stakeholders what meanings there are, and agree on alternative terms, one for each meaning, with those stakeholders. For example, while reviewing a rail transport operator's Requirements Specification, I discovered that "Line" had three subtly different meanings. The term was used to refer to (a) a corridor containing one or more tracks, (b) an individual track, or (c) a color-coded line on the published network map (which might include some or all of the tracks in one or more corridors). I obtained agreement to use "Line" only for the last meaning, and substitute "Corridor" and "Track" for the other two meanings.

If a Requirements Specification writer does not understand the business, there is the risk that the specification may contain overlapping generic and specific requirements. For example, the same rail transport operator Requirements Specification included the individual requirements depicted in Figure 7, during their capture in a spreadsheet. These appeared at various points in the spreadsheet; Figure 7 depicts them after intervening rows were hidden.

The specification writer had not realized that #54 and #207 were separate examples of the same requirement, or that #133 and #321 were separate examples of the same requirement. Furthermore, as they were unaware that the term "Decant Point" meant a facility for discharging wastewater, they did not know that all four of these were separate examples of one requirement, namely that some (but not all) locations on the network provided wastewater discharge facilities.

1	ID	Requirement
	54	54 Trains may discharge waste water at Central station
	133	133 Decant points are provided at Gosford and Newcastle Interchange
	207	207 Each Maintenance Centre provides waste water discharge facilities
	321	321 Decant points are provided at Katoomba and Lithgow

Figure 7: Overlapping requirements

Functional requirements and **nonfunctional requirements** should be listed separately. Functional requirements specify system behavior, while nonfunctional requirements specify such things as availability, capacity, compatibility, maintainability, manageability, performance, reliability, scalability, security, and usability.

Requirements Specifications are usually produced by business analysts. If the analyst understands the business's operations, terminology, issues, and problems, and follows the advice above, they can produce a quality Requirements Specification from which data and processes can be designed and built.

5.5.2 Software specifications

Typically, any new software is specified using separate documents to cover data, process, and business rules. Software specifications support off-the-shelf system selection and customization, system development, development of code to extract data from a system for data warehousing, and modifications to a system over its lifetime.

5.5.2.1 Data specifications

A data specification documents one of three models:
- A **business information model** lists the concepts of interest to the organization (typically referred to as **entity classes** or **entities**), with the

attributes of each concept and the **relationships** that exist between concepts. Its target audience is business stakeholders; the aim is to obtain their endorsement (after review and update as required) as an accurate model of the organization's information needs.

- Ideally, the target audience for a **logical data model** is application developers; it should therefore reflect the development environment they are using:
    - If that environment is object-oriented, the model should list the **object classes** against which developers will code, with the attributes of each object class and **associations** (relationships) that exist between object classes.
    - If developers are using embedded SQL to access **relational** or **object-relational** data, the model should list **tables**, each with **columns**, a **primary key**, **foreign keys** (if any), and **constraints**.
    - If the data medium is XML, the model should be the appropriate **XML schema**, with **elements**, **types**, **compositors**, and **attributes**.
- A **physical data model** lists the physical database objects; the target audience is database administrators and any developers using SQL for database access. For a relational or object-relational database, these are the same as those in a logical data model for embedded SQL. **Nontabular** database management systems[42] have a variety of other structures: a physical data model for such a system should reflect the structures available in that system.

Typically, only two models are produced: if the target database is relational or object-relational, the physical data model is the same as the logical data model with the addition of indexes and other performance improvement measures.

Any data model produced for a serious project will be an ongoing resource, as it will support not only ongoing use of the resulting database, but updates as

---

[42] These are often referred to as "Not only SQL" or "NoSQL" database management systems.

requirements evolve. It must therefore be managed as a data resource in its own right. These requirements, plus the fact that data modeling is a complex task, mean that any data specification document produced for human consumption is not an ideal source of truth for a data model.

Fortunately, there are various data modeling tools available to support data model development and management, with a variety of documentation functions. If the organization for which you are producing a data specification has not invested in such a tool, the best option is to install and use a freeware tool in which to develop the model. Most (if not all) data modeling tools only support two varieties of data model, often labeled "logical" and "physical". Depending on the tool, it may be feasible to create a business information model in the "logical data model" layer and a logical data model in the "physical data model" layer.

In the absence of a data modeling tool, you may consider using:

- a spreadsheet in which to record the components of the model (concepts, object classes, tables, attributes, columns, relationships, primary keys, foreign keys, constraints), or
- the database development and management tool that is (in most cases) bundled with the database management system.

The main disadvantages of using a spreadsheet are (a) the lack of constraints on data entry, (b) difficulty in generating a **database schema**, and (c) the need to use a separate diagramming tool to produce a data model diagram (which most stakeholders find essential as an aid to understanding). Even though a skilled user would be able to add constraints and schema generation functions, I do not recommend using a spreadsheet unless that is all that is available.

The main disadvantage of using a database documentation tool (as distinct from a data modeling tool) is that most (if not all) such tools document only the physical database rather than any business-level model.

Whatever model development environment you use, it should produce **data model diagrams** and **metadata**: definitions of (a) entity or object classes or tables, and (b) attributes or columns, along with statements of constraints such as mandatory attributes or columns. It should also be able to export diagrams and metadata in a form that can be embedded in a document published to relevant stakeholders.

At least one **technical writer** should be involved in the team crafting definitions, as **writer** or reviewer, applying the quality criteria listed in Section 4.2. If the data modeler(s) have any choice as to diagramming style, they should take account of the diagram quality criteria listed in Section 4.6.

Any large data model should be divided into **subject areas**, based on the organization's structure and/or functions, such as Customer Management, Product Management, Sales, Finance, and so on. The data specification document should reflect any such division: each subject area should be documented in a separate section, with subsections for the data model diagram and each entity (in which the entity and its attributes are defined). Given that some entities typically appear in multiple subject areas, it may be possible to organize the document so that any such entity is defined under only one subject area (the one in which it is the most important) with cross-references in the sections documenting other subject areas.

It is important to include in a Business Information Model document the requirement number(s) that each entity and/or attribute supports. If this information has been recorded in the data modeling tool, it can be exported with other metadata.

Data specifications should comply with the data modeling, database design, and data naming standards (if any) in use in the organization.

5.5.2.2 Process specifications

Processes are typically modeled using Business Process Modeling Notation (BPMN), which can be delivered to business stakeholders for review and developers for implementation. BPMN **activity diagrams** include:

- activities: tasks, which are atomic, and processes, which can be broken down into more detailed activities
- start, intermediate, and end events
- sequence flows
- decision points (or gateways) from which alternative or parallel sequence flows can branch
- message flows
- associations, including data associations
- data objects, inputs, outputs, and stores.

While these diagrams provide a useful overview of processes, a full description of a process requires a significant amount of textual material, including descriptions of process triggers and data effects, such as insertions, deletions, or updates. Most (if not all) BPMN tools support the recording of these.

Diagrams and any textual material should be able to be exported in a way that they can be embedded into a document that can be published to relevant stakeholders.

The technical writer's role should be to (a) support process modelers in the writing of process descriptions, (b) review the resulting descriptions, and (c) package the exported material into a document for business stakeholder consumption.

5.5.2.3 Business rule specifications

The business rule community have long advocated that business rules be specified using a **controlled natural language**, namely a subset of a natural language (such as English) in which both vocabulary and syntax (sentence forms) are restricted. The vocabulary (**noun phrases** and **verb phrases**) is typically drawn from a **business glossary** and the syntax from a set of standard templates. Rules of the same type should have a common syntax.

Each rule statement should be a grammatical sentence. That, with the use of business terminology, means that business stakeholders can readily interpret each rule statement.

As with data and processes, rule statements are best managed in a tool that manages templates and obtains terminology direct from the glossary, although many organizations have successfully managed their business rules in a word processor document or spreadsheet.

The quality of rule statements depends on the quality of both the templates and the rule statement generation process. However good these are, each set of rule statements generated should be subject to quality review, by both business stakeholders and a technical writer.

An important principle in rule statement syntax is that the subject of each rule statement must refer to the set of objects to be tested by that statement:

- For each rule requiring that an object have a value for a particular attribute, the statement subject must signify the object—rather than the attribute:
    - "Each Flight Booking Request for a Return Journey must specify exactly one Return Date."
    - "Each Employee has a Name, which must be recorded against that Employee."

- Statements prohibiting attribute values have a similar syntax but use "must not" rather than "must":
    - "A Flight Booking Request for a One-Way Journey must not specify a Return Date."
- If such a rule applies to a proper subset of the set of objects signified by the statement subject (as in the statements above about "Flight Booking Request"), a **prepositional phrase** is used to specify that subset[43]. This phrase may start with "for a" (as above) or "in which", as in:
    - "Each Road Vehicle in which Vehicle Type is Bus must specify exactly one Number of Standing Passengers."
- For each rule restricting the values that an attribute may have, the statement subject must signify the attribute:
    - "The Travel Class specified in each Flight Booking Request must be First, Business, Premium Economy, or Economy."
    - "The Number of Passengers specified in each Flight Booking Request must be between 1 and 9 inclusive."
    - "The Return Date (if any) specified in a Flight Booking Request must be no earlier than the Departure Date specified in that Flight Booking Request."
- For each rule governing a relationship, the statement subject must signify one of the objects participating in that relationship:
    - "Each Student must be the biological child of exactly two Responsible Adults, which may be omitted from the record of that Student."
- If such a rule applies to a proper subset of the set of objects signified by the statement subject, a **restrictive relative clause**[44] is used to specify that subset, as in:
    - "Each Tenancy that is not a Sole Tenancy must be held by two or more Parties, which must be recorded against that Tenancy."

---

[43] Or a **restrictive relative clause** (see later).

[44] Or a restrictive **prepositional phrase** (see above).

- Uniqueness rules use the word "different":
    - "Each combination of Person Name and Birth Date of a Traveler that is specified in the same Travel Insurance Request must be different."
    - "Each Customer must have a different Customer Number."

These examples represent only a small subset of the available rule statement types. My book *Data modeling for Quality* provides a more comprehensive coverage.

5.5.2.4 User interface specifications

A **user interface specification** typically uses **wireframes**: diagrams that depict the general layout of the elements of each page of a user interface, and contain:

- **window** properties, such as size, location, and title
- **input controls**, such as **text fields**; **checkboxes** and **radio buttons**; **dropdown lists** and **list boxes**; **date pickers** and **time pickers**; and **buttons**
- **navigational components**, such as **breadcrumbs**, **search fields**, **paginations**, **sliders**, **tags**, and **icons**
- **informational components**, such as **tooltips**, **progress bars**, **notifications**, **message boxes**, and **modal windows**.

These diagrams provide a useful visual guide to the user interface, but need accompanying descriptions, such as (a) the legends against each input control, (b) any constraints on what may be entered into each text field, (c) the allowed values in each dropdown list or list box, (d) the effect of clicking each button, and (e) navigation characteristics such as Tab and function key behavior.

Again, these are best managed in a dedicated tool that can export each wireframe and its accompanying descriptions in a form that can be embedded in a document that can be published to relevant stakeholders.

The technical writer's role should be to support user interface designers in the writing of these descriptions, review the resulting descriptions, and package the exported material into a document for business stakeholder consumption.

User interface specifications should comply with the user interface standard (if any) in use in the organization.

5.5.3 Change requests

A Change Request, usually raised by one or more users of a system, lists required changes to the behavior of that system, usually with an indication of the urgency of the change. If the users have correctly identified the relevant user interface screens and components, and clearly described the required changes, the Change Request can be lodged, given an identification number, and acted on.

However, before scheduling work on the requested change, it may be necessary for IT staff (business analyst, data modeler, process modeler, and/or user interface designer) to consult the users raising the Change Request, to verify precisely what they require and discuss options.

5.5.4 Release notices

Release Notices document the enhancements in a specific software release in terms of (a) changes in the behavior of a system, each cross-referenced to any Change Request that may have prompted the change, (b) the proposed release date, and (c) any actions required of users before, during, or immediately after rollout of the release.

5.5.5 Progress reports

Unless a project team uses collaboration software, team members may need to produce regular Progress Reports. Each report should include the following information:

- the period covered
- for each task not completed during the previous period:
  - the time spent (days or hours)
  - whether the task has now been completed
  - any dependencies: other tasks that must be completed or events that must occur (such as installation of enabling software) before this task can be completed
  - measures, such as the percentage complete, time remaining, and estimated completion date.

5.5.6 Meeting minutes

There should be minutes of each meeting at which any decisions are made about a project. Those minutes should include a statement of each decision made. For each decision, if there were any alternative points of view, there should be at least a summary of all points of view and the criteria considered in making the decision. The minutes should also include:

- a list of those present
- a list of any invitees who were unable to attend (to guard against any criticism of the decision based on failure to consult key stakeholders)
- the date and time of the meeting.

5.6 Organizational resources

Business Glossaries, Standards documents, and User Manuals are long-lasting organizational resources.

5.6.1 Business glossaries

A Business Glossary is a valuable resource for any organization. As a source of truth for the organization's approved terms and their meanings, it supports consistency in the organization's documents, data and process models, and user interfaces.

A glossary may be recorded in specialized software or in a shareable online word processor document. Each medium supports searches: a standard feature of glossary software is the use of hyperlinks by which to navigate cross-references, and these can also easily be added into a word processor document.

A glossary is a list of terms, each with a definition and any synonyms. Glossaries recorded as documents are usually organized alphabetically, in which case there should also be an entry for each nonapproved term, to support users searching for the correct term. For example, a user searching an Australian Land Registry glossary looking for the preferred term for a party owning real estate might check "owner" then "proprietor". The approved term is actually "tenant". To avoid users having to perform page-by-page searches of the entire glossary, it lists the synonyms "owner" and "proprietor", each with the notation "see Tenant".

Section 4.2 provides advice on crafting definitions.

5.6.2 Standards

Technical Standards documents include standards for data modeling, database design, data naming, coding, and user interfaces:

- Data modeling standards may include advice on assigning attributes to entities, normalization, relationship properties, and so on.
- **Database design standards** cover tables, column data types, column sequence, constraints (including primary and foreign keys and

uniqueness constraints), and primary key generation methods. Standards for specific metamodels may include additional information such as:

- standard columns in hub, satellite, link, point-in-time, and other tables in a data vault standard
- standard columns in fact and dimension tables, history recording in dimension tables, and dummy rows in dimension tables in a star schema standard.

- Data naming standards typically specify the rules governing the names of schemas, tables, columns, constraints, and other database artifacts, and may include rules governing names of
  - entity classes, attributes, and relationships in data models
  - elements, attributes, and user-defined types in XML schemas.

- User interface standards specify the visual and information characteristics of the user interfaces of the organization's systems:
  - Visual characteristics include screen layout, design of individual elements (in terms of fonts, colors, and so on).
  - Information characteristics include status notifications, alerts, error messages, and animation.

All standards should be clear and unambiguous to support consistency among data models, database designs, application code, and interfaces.

5.6.3   User manuals

The User Manual (or User Guide) for each system advises novice users how to log into and interact with that system to perform various tasks or obtain information. It also supports experienced users with information about functionality that they have never or rarely used.

A User Manual should adhere to the following principles:

- The hierarchy and sequence of sections should reflect the sets of tasks that users might perform. For example, in an order management system, some users might be responsible for adding, updating, or deleting product information, while others might wish to monitor sales figures, plan marketing campaigns or review campaign effectiveness. The guide should therefore have separate sections for data entry (with separate subsections for updating of product and campaign data) and information retrieval (with separate subsections for sales and campaigns). It should not be organized (as some guides are) as a hierarchic list of the contents of each menu or other element in each user interface window.

- Instructions to the reader as to what actions to perform should be in the **imperative mood**[45], as in "Click on the 'Save' button." Statements as to how the system responds to each user action should be in the **indicative mood**[46], as in "The system displays the customer's last three orders."

- Each dialog between a user and the system should be illustrated with screenshots from the system itself.

5.6.4 Standard Operating Procedures

A Standard Operating Procedures document lists the actions required in response to various events or situations. It should be organized as a hierarchy of event types, with actions documented in the **imperative mood**.

5.7 Office communications

While emails and messages sent via messaging apps are less formal than the other types of documents described in this chapter, any communication between project team members that is not of a personal nature should still be clear and unambiguous. One problem with emails is that busy recipients may overlook them, particularly if they receive many emails daily. Marking emails as "High Importance" or "Urgent" is not an effective solution (particularly if it is

---

[45] Defined in Section 9.6.6.2.
[46] See Section 9.6.6.

widespread practice in the organization). To ensure that recipients take note of any important email, **make clear in the subject line and first paragraph the purpose of each email**, that is, whether it is:

- a reply to a question previously asked by the recipient
- a question to which the sender wants an answer, or
- a request for the recipient to complete a task, such as read the email or a document, or provide information.

Each e-mail other than a reply to a question should specify in the subject line or first paragraph when the answer should be provided or the task completed.

If the recipient is to read a document attached to the email, write "**I attach**" rather than "**attached please find**". If they are to read a document not attached to the email, include a hyperlink to the document location.

Chapter 6. Crafting grammatical sentences

A **sentence** is a sequence of words with which to provide one or more readers with information or instructions or request information from them. To be effective, a sentence should obey grammatical rules, be unambiguous, and be easily understood. Any technical document should consist only of such sentences.[47]

The emphasis so far has been on writing easily understood sentences. Section 7.1 discusses how to avoid ambiguity. This chapter discusses what constitutes a grammatical sentence, in terms of:

- the various types of words (**word classes**)
- the assembly of words into **phrases**, **clauses**, and **sentences**
- how certain phrases and clauses can be used to refine the meaning of a sentence
- rules governing various combinations of words and phrases (**syntax** or grammar)
- punctuation and capitalization rules.

---

[47] Except in the **front matter** (defined in Section 4.10), headings, headers and footers, footnotes, definitions, bibliography, index, information organized into tables, and text in diagrams.

6.1 Grammatical terms

So far, this book has referred to various grammatical terms:

- **word classes**[48], such as **nouns, compound nouns, verbs, adjectives, adverbs, pronouns,** and **determiners**
- **phrase types**, such as **noun phrases, verb phrases,** and **prepositional phrases**[49]
- **clauses**.

These references have been in contexts that should make clear to the average reader what the term means. This chapter refers to these terms more frequently; since it uses these terms to state rules of grammar, this section lists them, as a reminder of the names and typical members of each class. Chapter 9 provides more details about each term.

6.1.1 Word classes

Members of a word class (or simply **class**) may be (a) single words, or (b) **compound words** acting as a single grammatical unit: these include **compound nouns** (such as "project manager"), **compound adjectives** (such as "up-to-date"), **compound prepositions** (such as "in front of"), and **phrasal verbs** (such as "roll back").

Each single or compound word belongs to at least one of the following classes:

- **nouns** (such as "system" or "product review"); **gerunds** (such as "completing") and **proper nouns** (such as "Bill Inmon") are specific subclasses

---

[48] Also known as **parts of speech**.
[49] There are other types of phrases, listed in Section 6.1.2.

- **determiners**, including **articles** ("a", "an", "the")
- **adjectives** (such as "modern" or "out of date"); specific subclasses are:
    - **gerundives** (such as "increasing")
    - **past participles** (such as "closed")
    - **ordinal numbers** (such as "first")
- **pronouns** (such as "it", "they", "that", "which")
- **prepositions** (such as "in", "during", "over", "because of")
- **verbs** (such as "create", "include"); specific subclasses are:
    - **primary auxiliaries** ("be", "have", "do")
    - **modals** ("can", "could", "may", "might", "must", "shall", "should", "will", "would")
    - **phrasal verbs** (such as "run out", "close down")
- **conjunctions** (such as "and", "or", "but", "if", "as soon as")
- **adverbs** (such as "consistently", "here", "often", "very", "later on").

There are words that belong to more than one class[50], including:

- noun/verb pairs (such as "detail", "impact", "load", "model")
- the '-ing' forms of verbs, which may behave as nouns (in which case they are **gerunds**) or adjectives (in which case they are **gerundives**)—for example, in "working from home", "working" acts as a noun, whereas, in "a working model", "working" acts as an adjective
- temporal prepositions that may also behave as conjunctions (such as "after", "before", "since", "until")
- locational prepositions that may also behave as adverbs (such as "above", "below").

---

[50] An alternative view is that there are identically spelled words of different classes.

Chapter 9 provides a definition of each of these classes, along with notes on the usage of words in that class, as well as details of how nouns and verbs **inflect** (change according to context).

6.1.2 Types of phrases

Each phrase belongs to one of the following types, each of which Section 9.9 discusses in detail:

- **noun phrases**, each formed from a noun along with an optional:
    - **determiner** and/or **adjective phrase**, as in "the current cycle"
    - **prepositional phrase**, as in "the issues in question"
    - **verb phrase**, as in "the tasks performed", "the issues outstanding", "the enhancements to be included", or
    - **relative clause**, as in "the errors that were detected"

  or a **pronoun** along with an optional:
    - **participial phrase**, as in "those rejected"
    - **prepositional phrase**, as in "those under review", or
    - **relative clause**, as in "those that were included"

- **verb phrases**, each formed from a verb:
    - **finite verb phrases**, such as "run", "ran", "has run", "must have run"
    - **present participial phrases**, using the '-ing' form of a verb, such as "running", "updating all tables"
    - **past participial phrases**, using the **past participle** of a verb, such as "deleted" or "written"
    - **infinitive phrases**, such as "to run" or "to be run"

- **adjective phrases**, each formed from an **adjective** along with an optional:
    - **adverb phrase**, as in "very fast", "large enough"
    - **prepositional phrase**, as in "effective under real-world conditions", or
    - **infinitive phrase**, as in "easy to check"

or a **comparative adjective** followed by "than" along with an optional:
- o **adjective phrase**, as in "slower than desirable"
- o **adverb phrase**, as in "slower than previously"
- o **noun phrase**, as in "cheaper than any alternative", or
- o **present participial phrase**, as in "faster than replacing all data"

- **adverb phrases**, each formed from an **adverb** along with an optional:
  - o **adverb**, as in "very efficiently", or
  - o **prepositional phrase**, as in "fortunately for the team"

- **prepositional phrases**, each formed from a **preposition** and a **noun phrase** preceded by an optional:
  - o **adverb phrase**, as in "soon after installing the software", or
  - o **present participial phrase**, as in "after completing the update"

- **absolute phrases**, each formed from a **noun phrase** followed by an:
  - o **adjective phrase**, as in "the rebuild complete", or
  - o **past participial phrase**, as in "the software installed".

6.1.3 Clauses

A **clause** consists of one or more **phrases** and contains at least one **verb**. Clauses are categorized in terms of:

- their content, as:
  - o **finite** (containing a **finite verb phrase**[51], such as "the enhancement has been tested"), or
  - o **nonfinite**, (containing a **present participle**, **past participle**, or **infinitive** but not a **finite verb phrase**), such as "passing all tests", "included in this release", or "to finish by midnight"

---

[51] Defined in Section 9.9.2.

- whether they are **independent** (able to stand alone as a complete sentence) or **dependent** (unable to stand alone).

An **independent clause** must (a) be a **finite clause**, and (b) not start with a **conjunction**[52] (such as "because" or "due to"). An independent clause can stand alone as a complete sentence, which may be:

- **declarative** (make an assertion), such as "The transaction is committed."
- **imperative** (issue a command or instruction), such as "Commit the transaction.", or
- **interrogative** (pose a question), such as "Has the transaction been committed?".

A **dependent** (or **subordinate**) **clause** cannot stand alone as a complete sentence, but may function as a **noun, adjective,** or **adverb** within a sentence. A dependent clause may be:

- **finite**, such as "that this occurred", "while the backup was running", or
- **nonfinite**, such as "to occur this often", "the backup having run".

A **finite dependent clause**:

- must start with a **subordinating conjunction**[53], unless the **subject** follows the **verb** due to dropping "if", as in "had it failed" instead of "if it had failed"
- may precede or follow the associated **independent clause**; if it precedes the independent clause, a comma is necessary, but if it follows the independent clause, no comma is necessary: "If it fails, it can be rerun." and "It can be rerun if it fails." are both correct.

---

[52] Defined in Section 9.7.
[53] Defined in Section 9.7.2.

6.1.3.1 Components of a clause

Each **independent clause** must contain not only a **finite verb phrase** but a **subject** (unless the clause is **imperative**, that is, a command) and a **direct object** (unless the verb is **intransitive**, as described in the next subsection). It may also contain additional phrases, such as:

- a **noun phrase** acting as the **indirect object**
- **adverb phrases**
- **prepositional phrases**
- **absolute phrases**
- other **verb phrases**.

The **subject** of a clause may be any of the following:

- a **noun phrase** referring to the person or thing that either:
    - acted as indicated by the **verb** in the clause, such as "the team" in "The team completed all enhancements.", or
    - was subject to the situation or relationship indicated by the verb and other parts of the sentence, such as "the data" in "The data is complete." or "The data is compromised."
- a **present participial phrase** and **noun phrase**, such as "completing the enhancement" in "Completing the enhancement was an essential task in this project."
- an **infinitive phrase** and **noun phrase**, such as "to attempt this migration" in "To attempt this migration would risk time and cost overruns."
- a **pronoun**, such as "we" in "We have completed data migration."

In "The team completed all enhancements.", "all enhancements" is the **direct object**, namely the person or thing acted on by the subject. The direct object may be:

- a **noun phrase**, as in "we completed the enhancement"
- a **present participial phrase**, as in "we completed enhancing the application"

- (after some verbs only) an **infinitive phrase**, as in "we intend to purchase this software".

Some verbs refer to situations or relationships rather than actions. Such verbs have subjects, but, rather than direct objects, they have **complements**. For example, "team leader" is the complement in "Ms Lee became the team leader this year." A complement may only be a **noun phrase** or **adjective phrase**.

6.1.3.2 Transitive and intransitive verbs

An **intransitive verb** is one that cannot be associated with a direct object or complement. For example, while "such systems exist" is valid, *"this system exists enhancements" is not.

A **transitive verb** must be associated with a direct object or complement. For example, while "we updated the data warehouse" is valid, *"we updated" is not.

Many verbs may be used either transitively or intransitively. For example, in "the machine stopped", "stopped" is intransitive whereas, in "the operator stopped the machine", "stopped" is transitive.

Some verbs have **indirect objects** as well as direct objects. For example, in "we have sent panel members our report" (or "we have sent our report to panel members"), "panel members" is the indirect object, and "our report" is the direct object. An indirect object may only be a **noun phrase** or **pronoun**.

The indirect object may either:

- follow the direct object (in which case it must be preceded by "to"), as in "we have sent it to them", or
- precede the direct object (in which case it is not preceded by "to"), but only if the direct object is a **noun phrase** rather than a pronoun, thus "we have sent them our report" is acceptable provided it is clear who "them" refers to, but *"we have sent panel members it" and *"we have sent them it" are not.

Not all verbs allow the indirect object to appear first: "give", "email", and "send" allow it, but not "deliver".

Some verbs (such as "provide") require different prepositions before the second object depending on whether that object is direct or indirect. Thus, "We will provide a report to stakeholders." and "We will provide stakeholders with a report."

6.1.3.3 Relative clauses

A **restrictive relative clause**:

- modifies the scope of the preceding **noun phrase**, whether that be:
    - the **subject** of the containing clause, as in "the employees who are qualified can sign on", or
    - an **object** of the containing clause, as in "we have reassigned the employees who are qualified" or "we have issued identity cards to the employees who are qualified"
- starts with "that" or a preposition followed by "which" (but not "which" alone) if the noun phrase refers to other than a person or persons,
- must not be preceded by a comma.

By contrast, a **nonrestrictive relative clause**:

- only provides more information about the preceding **noun phrase** rather than modify its scope, as in "the employees, who are qualified, have all signed on" or "we have reassigned the employees, who are qualified"
- starts with "which" or a preposition followed by "which" (but not "that") if the noun phrase refers to other than a person or persons
- must be preceded by a comma and, if not at the end of the sentence, followed by a comma, as in the first example above.

If the noun phrase refers to a person or persons, either type of relative clause starts with "who", "whom", "whose", or a preposition followed by "whom", as in "to whom access was granted".

6.1.3.4 Clause scope

A clause with a **plural subject noun phrase** and no **determiners**, such as "relational DBMSs do not perform adequately" implies that *all* relational DBMS perform inadequately. There are various ways of modifying such a clause to refer to only some of the items signified by the subject:

- Precede the subject noun phrase with:
    - an **adjective phrase** such as "early" or "pre-SQL99"
    - a **possessive noun phrase** such as "the organization's"
    - a **determiner** such as "these", but only if it is clear from preceding sentences what "these" refers to.
- Precede the subject noun with "the" and follow it with:
    - a **prepositional phrase** such as "in the company's technology stack"
    - a **restrictive relative clause** such as "that are used by the company"; note that "that are" may be omitted, to yield "used by the company".

6.2 Rules of grammar

This section sets out the main rules governing how the writer may combine words, phrases, and clauses into sentences. Supporters of the **descriptive** and **prescriptive** approaches to language regularly debate whether all these rules are appropriate or necessary.

The descriptive approach is the one adopted by most (if not all) dictionaries, which record all language usages encountered, often with little or no indication of whether a word or phrase is standard or nonstandard. A dictionary will therefore include words and phrases considered incorrect or inappropriate in standard or formal writing.

Technical documents are meant for managers and professionals, many of whom have grown up in a culture that prefers the use of standard and formal writing in the workplace. The writer of a technical document should meet the expectations of those who have such preferences, since doing so will not trouble any other readers who are not interested in, or even aware of, the rules of language.

This book, therefore, like those listed in the *Suggested Reading* list at the end of this book, is prescriptive, in that it sets out rules for which there is broad consensus. There are rules about which there is disagreement: Section 6.3 discusses these.

6.2.1 Sentence completeness

"The network connection failed." is a complete sentence, as are "The transaction was rolled back." and "Because the network connection failed, the transaction was rolled back." However, *"Because the network connection failed." is not a complete sentence.

Similarly, *"The network connection having failed." and *"Due to packet loss." are not complete sentences, even though "The network connection having failed, the transaction was rolled back." and "Due to packet loss, the transaction was rolled back." are both complete sentences.

Each complete sentence consists of one or more **clauses**, of which at least one must be a **finite clause**—one which contains a **finite verb phrase**[54] (such as "failed" or "was rolled back") without a preceding **subordinating conjunction**[55] such as "because".

---

[54] Defined in Section 9.9.2.
[55] Defined in Section 9.7.2.

6.2.2 Word order

While there is flexibility in the order in which one can include words in English sentences, there are many restrictions on word order.

6.2.2.1 Subject, verb, and objects

The rules for ordering the **subject**, **verb phrase**, and **objects** in a clause are as follows:

- The subject precedes the verb phrase, except in:
    - **interrogative clauses** posing direct questions, such as "Is the job finished?"
    - clauses starting with **negative prepositional phrases** or **conjunctions** such as "at no time", "nor", "not since", "not until", or "under no circumstances", as in "At no time was there any risk of data loss."
    - clauses following phrases or clauses starting with "only", as in "Only after the enhancement was implemented were we able to process these transactions."
    - clauses starting with "not only", such as "not only is this approach risky"
    - some clauses starting with "as", such as "this field may be left blank, as may the other date fields"
    - conditional clauses in which "if" is replaced, such as "had it succeeded" instead of "if it had succeeded".[56]
- Any object follows the verb phrase, as in "we have loaded the data", as does any **complement**, as in "The CIO is the appropriate authority."

---

[56] There are other clauses in which subject-verb inversion occurs in spoken English or in literature but not in technical or business writing.

- Any **indirect object** may appear either:
    - between the verb phrase and the **direct object**, as in "we have sent all team members an update", or
    - after a **preposition** following the direct object, as in "we have sent an update to all team members".

6.2.2.2 Adjectives

Adjectives may appear in two positions:

- A **predicative adjective** follows the verb phrase, as in "This data is invalid."
- An **attributive adjective** normally precedes the noun phrase it qualifies, as in "All invalid data has been corrected.", but:
    - may follow the noun in a **compound noun**[57], such as "Attorney General"
    - may follow a noun preceded by a **comparative adjective**[58], as in "the best person available"
    - may also qualify a **pronoun**[59] but must follow the pronoun, as in "those responsible"
    - may in some cases follow the qualified noun, but often with a meaning different from when used before the same noun. For example, "the concerned employees" means those employees who are worried, whereas "the employees concerned" means those employees who are involved. Similarly, "a responsible employee" means an employee who takes responsibility for their work, whereas "the employee responsible" means the employee who is responsible for something.

---

[57] Defined in Section 9.1.2.
[58] Defined in Section 9.3.4.
[59] Defined in Section 9.4.

Most native English speakers instinctively follow a specific sequence when using more than one attributive adjective to qualify a noun. For example, while "modern modeling tool" sounds right, *"modeling modern tool" does not. However, commentators differ in their assessments of that sequence:

- The majority state the sequence as: opinion, size, age, shape, color, origin, material, purpose.
- The British Council states the sequence as: general opinion, specific opinion, size, shape, age, color, origin, material.
- Others exclude purpose, reverse the sequence of age and shape, include type after material, or include condition after shape[60].

The Australian Government Style Manual takes a simpler approach, in which adjectives are:

- categorized as:
    - **evaluative**: denoting measurable features or opinions
    - **descriptive**: denoting observable but non-measurable features
    - **definitive**: denoting intrinsic features.
- written in the sequence evaluative, descriptive, definitive.

An advantage of this approach is that it simplifies decisions about whether (and where) to include commas between adjectives[61].

---

[60] These differences do not appear to reflect different US and UK usage.

[61] See Section 6.7.2.

6.2.2.3 Verb phrases

A multiword verb phrase may be split by the inclusion of one or more of the following (but only after the first word of the verb phrase)[62]:

- a **noun phrase** (as described in Section 6.1.2), as in "Will this situation occur?", "Has it occurred previously?", "under no circumstances can this be allowed to occur"
- "not", as in "It has not occurred previously."
- an **adverb phrase**, as in "It has previously occurred."
- a **prepositional phrase**, as in "It has, in any case, occurred previously."
- a **dependent clause**, as in "It has, as we reported, occurred frequently."

If more than one phrase or clause is used to split a verb phrase, the sequence should be (1) noun phrase, (2) "not", (3) prepositional phrase, (4) dependent clause, (5) adverb phrase, as in "has it not arisen previously?", "it has not previously arisen", or "it has not, to the best of our knowledge, arisen previously".

6.2.2.4 Phrasal verbs

A **phrasal verb** is a verb followed by an **adverb** (such as "put together") or a **preposition** (such as "call for"). Other phrasal verbs that might be found in technical or business writing include "back up", "break down", "build in", "call off", "carry on", "check out", "fall through", "follow up", "go ahead", and "hand over".

Some transitive phrasal verbs ending with an adverb may be written with the adverb before or after the **direct object**, as in "leave out the details" and "leave the details out". This is not possible with phrasal verbs ending with a **preposition**.

---

[62] Note that some writers advise against such verb splitting but I can find no authoritative source that condemns it.

For example, "call for a different approach" cannot be rephrased *"call a different approach for". An adverb of a phrasal verb should not be written after a long direct object. For example, while "We have rolled out version 3.2 of the online timetable management software." is understandable, *"We have rolled version 3.2 of the online timetable management software out." is not.

6.2.2.5   Adverb phrases

An **adverb phrase** may appear in various locations in a clause but there are rules governing where an adverb phrase may appear:

- If the verb phrase is **present** or **simple past**, the adverb phrase may appear before the verb phrase (as in "we often see this error") or after any objects (as in "we see this error often"), but not between the verb phrase and any objects, as in *"we see often this error".
- If the verb phrase starts with a form of "have", "be", "do", and/or a **modal**:
    - the adverb phrase may appear after the verb phrase (as in "we have seen this error often"), but not before the verb phrase (as in *"we often have seen this error")
    - some adverb phrases may appear after the first word of the verb phrase (as in "we have often seen this error"), but not all adverb phrases may split a verb phrase in this way. For example, while "it has previously arisen" and "it has arisen previously" are both valid, *"it has before arisen" should be "it has arisen before". Avoid splitting a verb phrase with adverb phrases of three or more words.
- An adverb phrase may always follow an **infinitive phrase**, as in "We intend to remedy this immediately." Unless there is a ban on **split**

infinitives[63], the adverb phrase may alternatively appear between "to" and the verb **base form**[64], as in "we intend to immediately remedy this".

Moving an adverb phrase may change the meaning of a clause. For example:

- Compare "we deliberately did not delete the data", "we did not deliberately delete the data", and "we did not delete the data deliberately". The first clause asserts that (a) the data was not deleted and (b) that was deliberate. The second and third assert that, if the data was deleted, it was not deliberate. However, "we deliberately deleted the data" and "we deleted the data deliberately" have the same meaning.
- The adverb "still" may change the meaning of a sentence depending on its location:
  - "if we were to proceed, data quality would be still worse than previously" means that proceeding would exacerbate the data quality issue
  - "if we were to proceed, data quality would still be worse than previously" means that proceeding would have little or no effect on data quality.
- The adverb "only" may change the meaning of a sentence depending on its location:
  - "only the manager had read access to this table" means no-one other than the manager could read the table
  - "the only manager had read access to this table" means that there is only one manager, who is among those who can read the table
  - "the manager only had read access to this table", "the manager had only read access to this table", and "the manager had read-only access to this table" each mean that the manager cannot update the table

---

[63] See Section 6.3.1.

[64] Defined in Section 9.6.1.

o "the manager had read access only to this table", "the manager had read access to only this table", and "the manager had read access to this table only" mean that this is the only table the manager can read.

6.2.2.6 Determiners

Some **determiners** may move from the beginning of the **subject noun phrase** to after the first verb in the verb phrase, as in "The enhanced modules are all installed." instead of "All the enhanced modules are installed."

6.2.2.7 Prepositional phrases

Some, but not all, prepositional phrases may be moved within a sentence. Thus "Replication of the previous month's data from the data vault to the data marts occurs on the first day of each month." may be alternatively worded "Replication of the previous month's data to the data marts from the data vault occurs on the first day of each month." or "Replication from the data vault to the data marts of the previous month's data occurs on the first day of each month."

6.2.3 Conjoined clauses

Two clauses may be joined by a **conjunction** such as "and", as in "In May 2019, the development team completed all Version 2.4 enhancements and the test team completed testing of all Version 2.3 enhancements." In this case, the clauses may be swapped, yielding "In May 2019, the test team completed testing of all Version 2.3 enhancements and the development team completed all Version 2.4 enhancements." Such swaps do not always make sense, particularly if there is a dependency or time difference between the actions or events described. For example, while "The development team completed all enhancements and the test team tested them." makes sense, !"The test team tested all enhancements and the development team completed them." does not make sense.

Note that, if the clauses are swapped and the second clause includes a **pronoun** referring to a **noun phrase** in the first clause, the clauses are not swapped verbatim. Thus, "Our technical writer has written the text for this specification and our data modeler has produced the diagrams for it." may be rephrased "Our data modeler has produced the diagrams for this specification and our technical writer has written the text for it."

If both clauses have the same **subject**, it may be omitted in the second clause rather than being replaced by a pronoun. For example, "The development team have completed all Version 2.4 enhancements and the development team have started on Version 2.5 enhancements." could be written as either:

- "The development team have completed all Version 2.4 enhancements and they have started on Version 2.5 enhancements." (the subject has been replaced by **pronoun**), or
- "The development team have completed all Version 2.4 enhancements and have started on Version 2.5 enhancements." (the subject has been omitted).

Again, if these clauses were swapped, omission, like replacement by a pronoun, may only occur in the second clause.

6.2.3.1 Conjunction behavior

In all these clause swaps, "and" remains between the two clauses. The conjunctions "but", "or", "whereas", and "yet" also remain between the clauses.

By contrast, "if" moves with the clause it introduces. For example, "If any mandatory field is omitted, an error message is displayed." may alternatively be written "An error message is displayed if any mandatory field is omitted." A comma is required between the clauses if there is no conjunction in that position, but not required if there is a conjunction.

Other conjunctions move with the following clause, the most common of which are listed here (grouped by their semantic functions):

- reason: "because", "in order that", "since", "so that"
- comparison: "although", "as much as", "even though", "though"
- condition: "even if", "in case", "only if", "provided", "unless", "whether or not"
- place: "where", "wherever"
- time: "after", "as", "as soon as", "as long as", "before", "by the time", "every time", "now that", "once", "until", "when", "whenever".

There are some conjunctions with specific behavior:

- "while" may either remain between the clauses or move with the following clause—for example, "The project team started documentation while they completed testing." could be rephrased "The project team completed testing while they started documentation." or "While the project team completed testing, they started documentation."
- Unlike "so that", "so" does not move with the following clause, but clause swapping would change the meaning, as described in Section 6.2.3.3
- "as though" and "except that" do not allow clause swapping.[65]

6.2.3.2   Conjunctions and nonfinite verb phrases

Some conjunctions may be followed by a **present participial phrase**[66], as in "The project team started documentation while completing testing." As well as "while", others that allow this include "after", "although", "before", "if", "since", "unless", "when", and "where".

---

[65] Except in poetry or other literary works.
[66] Defined in Section 9.9.3.1.

The conjunctions "so as" and "in order" must be followed by an **infinitive phrase**[67], as in "This constraint was added so as to prevent invalid data."

6.2.3.3 Conjunction semantics

There is a subtle difference between "so" and "so that":

- "Constraints have been implemented so that data quality should improve." implies that the motivation for implementing constraints was data quality improvement.
- "Constraints have been implemented, so data quality should improve." implies that data quality improvement will be a consequence of implementing constraints but not necessarily the motivation.

There are semantic differences between "if", "only if", and "if and only if":

- "A 10% discount is applied if the order exceeds $US100." means the discount is applied to all orders over $US100 and may be applied to other orders.
- "A 10% discount is applied only if the order exceeds $US100." means the discount may be applied to orders over $US100 but is not applied to other orders.
- "A 10% discount is applied if and only if the order exceeds $US100." means the discount is applied to all orders over $US100 and is not applied to other orders.

6.2.4 Subject-verb agreement

In the **simple present, present perfect** and corresponding **progressive tenses**[68] different verb forms are required after **singular** and **plural nouns**. Compare "the test is complete" and "the tests are complete".

---

[67] Defined in Section 9.9.3.3.
[68] Defined in Section 9.6.3.5.

Some **collective nouns** (such as "board", "committee", "company", "department", "government", "group", "panel", "team") may be treated as either singular or plural:

- If members of the collection are acting in unison, use a **singular** verb, as in "The board is celebrating the success of the project."
- If they are acting individually, either:
    - use a **plural** verb, as in "The board are reviewing our report." or
    - add the word "members", as in "The board members are reviewing our report."

However, other collective nouns (such as "staff") may only be treated as plural: *"All staff has completed the required training." should be "All staff have completed the required training."

The nouns "data" and "media", both technically plural, are usually treated as singular **mass nouns**[69]. Treat each of these nouns consistently within one document or set of related documents. However, most (if not all) editors and style guides now treat "agenda" (technically plural) as singular.

A **proper noun** may refer to a single composite entity instance but be in plural form. For example, it is legitimate to write "the United States is our biggest market" rather than *"the United States are our biggest market".

The rules are more complex for **pronouns**:

- "he", "she", "it", "this", "that", "anybody", "anyone", "everybody", "everyone", "nobody", "no one"[70], "somebody", "someone" "anything", "everything", "nothing", "something", "another", "each", "either", "enough",

---

[69] Defined in Section 6.2.4.

[70] "No-one" is acceptable in most communities, but "noone" is universally regarded as incorrect.

"neither", "the other", "less", "little", and "much" may only appear before a **singular** verb form, such as "is" or "has"

- "we", "you", "they", "these", "those", "others", "a few", "both", "few", "fewer" "many", and "several" may only precede a **plural** verb form, such as "are" or "have"
- "I" may only precede a **plural** verb form (such as "have") except with the verb "be", for which the form after "I" is "am"
- "none" may precede either a **singular** or **plural** verb form, thus "none is" and "none are" are both acceptable
- "there" precedes a **singular** verb form before a singular noun phrase and a **plural** verb before a plural noun phrase, as in "there is a new version" and "there are more users"
- "that" precedes a **singular** verb form after a singular noun phrase and a **plural** verb form after a plural noun phrase, as in "there are sections that are not complete" and "there is one section that is not complete"
- "which" acts like "that" but also precedes a **singular** verb form when it refers to the entire preceding clause, as in "there are more concurrent processes, which has impacted response times"
- "who" precedes a **plural** verb form if it follows a plural noun phrase, as in "the users who have left" but not otherwise: *"to establish who use this system" is incorrect.

Section 7.3 lists some common violations of these rules.

6.2.5 Determiner-noun agreement

A **count noun** (or **countable noun**) is one that may correctly appear after the word "each". For example, it makes sense to write "each customer" or "each order", whereas it does not make sense to write *"each information" or *"each governance". Thus, "customer" and "order" are count nouns, whereas "information" and "governance" are **mass nouns** (or **noncountable nouns**). Other common mass nouns are "equipment", "excellence", "management", "progress", and "traffic".

Some **determiners** (such as "a", "an", "this", "that", "each", or "less") may only appear before a **singular** noun. Of these, "a", "an", "each", and "several" may only appear before **count** nouns. For example, *"an information" makes no sense.

In particular, "either" and "neither":

- may only be used to signify one or none of two possibilities (if there are more than two possibilities, use "any" or "no", as in "any table" or "no table")
- may only appear:
    - immediately before a **singular** noun, as in "either table"
    - before a **plural** noun preceded by "of the", as in "neither of the tables"
    - before a **singular** or **plural** noun followed by "or" or "nor", as in "either the primary keys or the uniqueness constraints" or "neither developers nor testers".

The determiner "less" should only appear before mass nouns, such as "time" or "information", or measurements (when used with "than"), as in "less than two months".[71] For example, write "fewer employees" rather than *"less employees". However, both "less than 30% of employees" and "fewer than 30% of employees" are acceptable. The use of "or less" after a number (as in "ten or less") or measurement (as in "30 days or less") is also acceptable, although some prefer "or fewer" after a number. Immediately after a number other than one, there is a

---

[71] Some dictionaries cite the use of "less" before count nouns, but this is not favored in business or technical writing.

preference for "fewer" (as in "three fewer") over "less", but "less" is acceptable after "one" (as in "one less issue").

The determiners "these", "those", "both", "many", "few", "fewer" may only appear before **plural** nouns.

The determiners "all", "some", "more", "most" may appear before **mass** nouns or **plural count** nouns, while "no" may appear before any type of noun.

The **cardinal number** "one" may only appear before a **singular count** noun, while "two", "three" (and so on) may only appear before **plural count** nouns.

Determiners such as "one or more", "two or more", "at least two", and "at least three" may only appear before **plural count** nouns, but "at least one" (like "at most one") may only appear before a **singular count** noun.

At least one determiner must appear before a **singular count** noun. Thus *"System is installed." is incorrect. A **plural** noun may appear without any determiner, although the resulting sentence may be too much of a generalization, as in "Requirements are mandatory."

The determiners "former" and "latter" should only be used to refer to one of two items previously mentioned. If more than two items have previously been mentioned, use "first" or "last". This applies also to the use of these words as **pronouns**. Thus *"Primary keys can be generated by a hash function, a database-generated sequence number, or an RFC 4122-compliant identifier; of these the latter is preferred." is incorrect.

6.2.6 Pronoun rules

Use the **subject** form of a personal pronoun (such as "he", "she", or "they") for the **subject** of a clause and the **object** form (such as "him", "her", or "them") for the direct or indirect **object** of a clause or after any **preposition**. Use the **object** form for any pronoun in a **series** after a preposition, as in "This was a successful outcome for his colleagues and him." rather than *"This was a successful outcome for his colleagues and he."

If the writer wishes to refer to themself using a pronoun, they should use "I" for the subject and "me" otherwise, or use "the writer" as subject, object, or after a preposition.

The pronouns "either" and "neither":

- may only be used to signify one or none of two possibilities (if there are more than two possibilities, use "any" or "none")
- when used as the subject, should be followed by a singular verb, as in "either is possible"

6.2.7 Preposition rules

Most verbs, nouns and adjectives may only be legitimately followed by certain prepositions. For example, we write "comply with" or "compliance with" a regulation rather than *"comply to" or *"compliance for". These combinations are so numerous as to be outside the scope of this book. If you are in doubt as to the appropriate preposition to use after a particular verb, noun, or adjective, search online for "verb prepositions", "noun prepositions", or "adjective prepositions".

The preposition "between" is unique in that it requires either:

- two objects separated by "and", as in "between 2008 and 2012", or
- a plural object, as in "between backups".

6.2.8 Comparative and superlative adjectives

When using an adjective to compare only two alternatives, use the **comparative** rather than the **superlative**.[72] Thus "the better of the two options" is correct whereas *"the best of the two options" is not. Similarly, "the best of the three options" is correct whereas *"the better of the three options" is not.

A superlative adjective must always be preceded by "the" rather than "a" or "an". Thus "the best option" is correct whereas *"a best option" is not.

6.3 Contentious rules

While the rules of grammar and writing in both US and UK Standard English are well-documented, there are three so-called rules that are hard to justify, and another rule that is more complex than it might appear at first glance.

6.3.1 Splitting the infinitive

This term refers to inserting one or more words between "to" and the infinitive form of a verb, as in "to repeatedly fail". Although various authorities have ruled that such a construction is invalid in Standard English, modern guides to English usage do not object to it.

Some writers avoid splitting other multiword verb phrases, as in "It has regularly caused customer data to be corrupted." I can find no authoritative source that condemns this practice.

---

[72] Comparatives and superlatives are formed as detailed in Table 14 in Section 9.3.4.

6.3.2 Ending a sentence with a preposition

Again, although various authorities have ruled that placing a preposition at the end of a sentence is invalid in Standard English, modern guides to English usage do not object to it. Indeed, there are sentences in which such a construction is preferable to the alternative. For example, "This is the issue that we are concerned about." rather than "This is the issue about which we are concerned."

6.3.3 Using the passive voice

Many authoritative sources advocate the use of the active rather than the passive voice. However, the passive voice may be useful in technical writing:

- It may make a sentence more concise, particularly one which describes an action that anyone may take. For example, "A technical writer may use the passive voice where appropriate." may be shortened to "One may use the passive voice where appropriate." or "The passive voice may be used where appropriate." While both these alternatives save two words, sentences with the impersonal pronoun "one" may seem stilted.
- It is useful:
    - to maintain sentence flow—for example, "The passive voice is useful in technical writing. It may be used to make a sentence more concise." flows better than "The passive voice is useful in technical writing. The writer may use it to make a sentence more concise." since both sentences have the same **subject**.
    - when the **actor** is unknown or irrelevant, as in "Commuters were delayed by an average of 30 minutes today."
    - when it is better not to identify the actor, as in "The database was loaded with incorrect data."
    - when the impact of the action is more important than the actor, as in "Many customers have been overcharged."

That said, use the active voice wherever it results in a more concise sentence.

6.3.4 The Oxford comma

A **serial comma** (or **Oxford comma**) is a comma placed immediately before "and" or "or" in a list of three or more items. Many US style guides insist on it in all circumstances while others (including the Associated Press Stylebook, the Australian Government Style Manual, the Canadian Press Stylebook, and recent issues of the New Oxford Style Manual) recommend using a serial comma to add clarity only in specific circumstances.

Consider "The report was sent to Ms Ali, the CIO and the Project Manager." It is just possible that Ms Ali is both the CIO and the Project Manager, the report was sent to her, and the writer felt it was appropriate to list her roles. Alternatively (and more likely), Ms Ali, the CIO, and the Project Manager are three different people. Including a serial comma before "and" makes clear that they are three different people. If Ms Ali is the sole recipient, the sentence will have to be rephrased, either "The report was sent to Ms Ali, who is both CIO and Project Manager." or "The report was sent to CIO and Project Manager Ms Ali."

Now consider "The review panel consists of project team members, Mr Singh and Ms Cohen." This is ambiguous because it is not clear whether the panel consists of (a) just the two people mentioned (who happen to be project team members) or (b) the two people mentioned plus project team members. Including a serial comma before "and" makes clear that the second interpretation is intended. If the first interpretation is intended, there should be no comma: "The review panel consists of project team members Mr Singh and Ms Cohen."

The major argument against dogmatic use of the serial comma is that commas have multiple purposes, in particular setting off parenthetical content. Consider the sentence "The review panel consists of the CIO, Mr Singh, and Ms Cohen." This may be interpreted in two ways: the panel consists either of two people—Singh (who is the CIO) and Cohen—or three people. Removing the serial comma yields "The review panel consists of the CIO, Mr Singh and Ms Cohen." which may only be interpreted in one way: the panel consists of three people. If the panel consists of two people, the sentence should be recast as "The review panel consists of the CIO (Mr Singh) and Ms Cohen."

6.4 Rules governing series

A **series**[73] is two or more items listed either within a single sentence or separated in the form of a **bulleted** or **numbered list**. Do not add a number or bullet to a single paragraph: there should always be at least two such paragraphs.

6.4.1 Consistency

Items in a series should all be of the same type, for example:

- all noun phrases, as in "developers, database administrators, and testers"
- all verb phrases, as in "extract, transform, and load".

A **bulleted** or **numbered list** must be introduced using either (a) a complete sentence (such as "The following options are available:") or (b) a **sentence stub** (such as "Available options include:"). There is no need to include the number of items in the list; it may change, and you may forget to update it.

Each item in an **inline series** must form a grammatical sentence with whatever precedes the first item. For example, items (b) and (c) in *"This is true whether they are (a) created by an external authority, (b) by a nominated authority within the enterprise, or (c) automatically by a system." fail this test. This sentence should read "This is true whether they are created (a) by an external authority, (b) by a nominated authority within the enterprise, or (c) automatically by a system."

---

[73] Discussed in detail in Section 4.1.

Similarly, each item in a **bulleted** or **numbered list** introduced by a sentence stub must form a grammatical sentence with the sentence stub. The final item in Figure 8 fails this test.

*This version features:
- enhanced security
- additional mapping functionality, and
- supports more simultaneous users.

Figure 8: A malformed list

6.4.2 Conjunction use

An **inline series** must include "and" or "or" before the last item. A **bulleted** or **numbered list** of phrases (but not a list of sentences) may at the writer's discretion include "and" or "or" after the last but one item (separated from it by a comma), as in Figure 8.

6.4.3 Series Punctuation

- An **inline series** without distinguishing letters or numbers:
    - requires no punctuation if there are only two items
    - requires commas between consecutive items and "and" or "or" before the last item if there are more than two items.

- An **inline series** with distinguishing letters or numbers requires commas between consecutive items and "and" or "or" before the last item.

- Depending on the convention being followed and the impact on meaning or ambiguity[74], a comma may precede "and" or "or".

---

[74] See Section 6.3.4 for an example where the inclusion of a comma before "and" or "or" may introduce ambiguity.

- The sentence or sentence stub introducing a **bulleted** or **numbered list** should end with a colon rather than a period (full stop).
- The last item in a **bulleted** or **numbered list** should end with a period.
- The remaining items in a **bulleted** or **numbered list** should each end with a period if and only if they are complete sentences.

6.5 Indefinite articles

The rules for using "a" or "an" are based on the initial sound of the following word rather than its initial letter, as listed in Table 9.

Before words starting with	Use	Examples
'a', 'i'	an	
'u' with opening 'y' sound	a	a unit
'u' without opening 'y' sound	an	an upload
'o' with opening 'w' sound	a	a one-way street
'o' without opening 'w' sound	an	an offset
'eu'	a	a European policy
'e' (not 'eu')	an	an element
'h' (silent)	an	an honest appraisal
'h' (sounded)[75]	a	a house
'y' with 'i' sound	an	an Yttrium deposit
'y' without 'i' sound	a	a yellow highlight
'f', 'l', 'm', 'n', 'r', 's', 'x' (letter name)	an	an x-ray
any other letter	a	

Table 9: Indefinite articles

---

[75] It has been acceptable in some circles to also use "an" before a word starting with an aspirate (non-silent) 'h' if the first syllable of that word is unstressed, as in "an historic event" but most style guides do not recommend this.

6.6 Forming the possessive of a long compound noun

Use "of" rather than "'s" for the **possessive** form of a long **compound noun**. For example, "the director of the Center for Politics at the University of Virginia" rather than !"the Center for Politics at the University of Virginia's director".

6.7 Punctuation

This section covers the valid uses of each punctuation mark.

6.7.1 Periods / full stops

The **period** (**full stop** in UK terminology) has various uses:

- at the end of each **declarative** or **imperative** sentence[76], except one that introduces a **bulleted** or **numbered list** (which should be terminated using a colon)
- at the end of (or within) **initialisms** or other **abbreviations**[77], depending on the style guide being followed:
    - Section 4.5.1 provides guidance on the use of periods after abbreviated month or day names.
    - Section 4.5.2 provides guidance on the use of periods in "am" and "pm" in times of day.
- after persons' abbreviated titles (as in "Ms." and "Dr."):
    - always in US usage
    - in UK usage, only if the last letter of the abbreviation is different to that of the full form, thus "Mr" but "Prof."

---

[76] Defined in Section 9.6.6.
[77] See Section 4.4.

- optionally after a person's initials, as in "Arthur C Clarke" or "Arthur C. Clarke":
    - periods are more common in US than UK usage
    - be consistent in including or omitting periods
- as decimal points in numerals.

If a sentence ends with an abbreviation, use only a single period to complete both the abbreviation and the sentence.

Do not include a period at the end of a heading.

6.7.2 Commas

Commas have a wide variety of uses, so writers must take care when using them. Use a comma:

- before a **coordinating conjunction** ("and", "but", "for", "or", "nor", "so", or "yet") between **independent clauses**
- after an introductory word or phrase that precedes the **main clause**, as in "However, this is no longer a problem." and "Without careful key design, referential integrity and data quality may be compromised."
- after a **dependent clause** that precedes the main clause, as in "If the End Date is unknown, it may be left blank."
- before or after **quoted material**, as described in Section 6.7.14
- before and after:
    - a **parenthetical expression** (a word, phrase, or clause that is not essential to the meaning of the sentence), as in "this has, however, arisen previously", "it has, in any case, arisen previously", and "it has, as we have seen, arisen previously", except when the expression follows a **coordinating conjunction** between **independent clauses**, in which case there is no comma between the conjunction and the expression: for example, "the data was checked, but as we predicted, some errors slipped through"

- a **nondefining clause**[78], as in "this data, which was loaded yesterday, is corrupt"; by contrast, a **defining clause**[79] should not be set off with commas, thus "the data that was loaded yesterday is corrupt"
- an **appositive** (an explanatory word or phrase after a noun), as in "One of our largest suppliers, XYZ, has increased its market share." or "XYZ, one of our largest suppliers, has increased its market share." Note that the second comma may be omitted with only a slight change of meaning, as in "One of our largest suppliers, XYZ has increased its market share." However, the following constructions are invalid:
  - *"One of our largest suppliers XYZ, has increased its market share."
  - *"XYZ one of our largest suppliers, has increased its market share."
  - *"XYZ, one of our largest suppliers has increased its market share."

- to separate three or more words or phrases written in a **series**, as in "this solution is fit for purpose, easy to maintain, and inexpensive"; Section 6.3.4 provides guidance as to whether there should be a comma before "and" or "or"

- to separate groups of three digits in numbers greater than 999, as in "1,024"

- in some dates, as described in Section 4.5.1

- after "e.g." or "i.e." (US usage only)

- between a placename and the name or abbreviation of the state, province, territory, or country, as in "London, UK", as well as after the state, province, territory, or country designator if the sentence continues, thus "As well as our head office in Seattle, WA, we have branches in all states."

---

[78] A **nondefining clause** is one that only provides additional information about a noun phrase.

[79] A **defining clause** is one that limits a noun phrase to a specific subset, in this case only the data loaded yesterday.

- wherever necessary to prevent confusion or misreading.

A comma should also be used to separate two or more **coordinate adjectives** (adjectives of the same category as defined in Section 6.2.2.2) that describe the same noun, as in "this is an effective, inexpensive solution"; if you are unsure about whether to use a comma in this situation, there are two tests you can apply:

- Try writing "and" between them: if it makes sense, as in "effective and inexpensive solution", a comma should be included, but if it does not, as in *"an inexpensive and relational data platform", a comma should not be included.
- Try reversing the order of the adjectives: if it makes sense, as in "inexpensive, effective solution", a comma should be included, but if it does not, as in *"relational modern data platform", a comma should not be included.

Do not use a comma:

- before "however", "therefore", "hence", "consequently", "nevertheless", or "thus" between two clauses (use a semicolon instead)
- between the **subject** and **verb** in a clause, however long the subject, as in *"the loading of the rest of yesterday's data, was completed in one hour"
- before or after relative clauses beginning with "that" after nouns, as in *"the data, that was corrupted, has been corrected"
- after verbs expressing mental action, as in *"we have decided, to adopt a different approach"
- between two independent clauses without an intervening conjunction, as in *"the enhancements have been tested, they have now been implemented"[80]

---

[80] The use of a comma in this situation is known as a **comma splice**.

Since commas have so many uses, a sentence may have many of them. In this situation, it may be better to replace some of them with other parenthetical separators such as parentheses or dashes. For example, "Implementation of constraints—such as primary keys, foreign keys, and uniqueness constraints—is the responsibility of the database administrator."

6.7.3 Colons

Use a colon:

- between two independent clauses where the second provides detail about the first, as in "the data load failed for one reason: it was not checked"; do not use a coordinating conjunction (such as "and", "or", or "but") after the colon
- before quoted material, after an independent clause, as described in Section 6.7.14
- between an abbreviation and its full form in an abbreviation list, as in "DBMS: Database management system"
- between a term and its meaning in a glossary or a list of categories, as in "primary key: one or more columns with different values in each row of a table, used to distinguish one row from another"
- as an hour/minute/second separator in times, as in "17:30"
- to terminate a sentence that introduces a **bulleted** or **numbered list**, such as "Use a colon:" here
- between the number and caption to a table or figure, as in "Table 1: data types".

Do not use a colon at the end of a heading.

6.7.4 Semicolons

Use a semicolon:

- between two independent clauses, as in "some information may be omitted; it will be captured later"[81]; do not use a coordinating conjunction (such as "and", "or", or "but") after the semicolon
- in a two-level **inline series**, as in "business stakeholders: system users and their managers; the design team: data, process, and rules modelers; and the build team: database administrators and developers".

6.7.5 Parentheses

Use parentheses to enclose:

- one or more words that provide additional but nonessential information, as in "This approach (in our opinion) poses the risk of more frequent outages."
- one or more letters that form an optional part of a word, as in "The developer(s) must take these constraints into account."

For each opening parenthesis there must be a corresponding closing parenthesis.

When enclosing a complete sentence in parentheses, place that sentence's closing period before the closing parenthesis, as in "The system must check for duplicate primary keys. (This is because the DBMS has not been configured to perform such checks.)". When enclosing a word or phrase at the end of a sentence in parentheses, place the closing period after the closing parenthesis, as in "The system performs integrity checks (since the DBMS has not been configured to do so)."

---

[81] However, when the second clause provides detail about the first clause, use a colon.

6.7.6 Square brackets

Square brackets should only be used in technical or business writing for one purpose (other than in mathematical formulae): to mark replacement text in a quotation, as described in Section 4.3. For each opening bracket ("[") there must be a corresponding closing bracket ("]").

6.7.7 Dashes

There are two types of dashes: the **em dash** ("—") and the **en dash** ("–"), so named because their widths are those of the letters "m" and "n" respectively.

One may use an em dash:

- instead of a comma or parenthesis to delimit a **parenthetical expression** (a word, phrase, or clause that is not essential to the meaning of the sentence), as in "It has—as we predicted—led to data corruption."
- in particular, to delimit a **parenthetical expression** containing another delimited by parentheses, as in "All database components—tables (with columns, data types, and constraints) and stored procedures— have been created."
- to delimit an **inline series**, as in "All database components—schemas, tables, columns, and constraints—are named to comply with the standards."
- before explanatory material introduced by "for example" or "that is", as in "A business key should be defined for each table—for example, the IATA airline or airport code."
- instead of a colon or semicolon to separate **independent clauses**, as in "The data has been loaded—no data was rejected."

One may use an en dash instead of "to":

- between dates and times, as in "The office will be closed December 25–January 2" or "The system will be offline 02:00–03:00."; note that "from" (necessary if "to" were used) should not be used before a date or time range using a dash

- between placenames, as in "The Sydney–Melbourne service."

These are longer than hyphens, which should not be used in place of dashes in any of the above situations.

6.7.8 Ellipses

The ellipsis[82] symbol ("…") should only be used in technical or business writing for one purpose: to indicate text omitted from within a quotation, as in "He replied that the system was … not fit for purpose." where the quoted statement included other words between "was" and "not" which the writer considers irrelevant.

6.7.9 Quotation marks

Use quotation marks before and after:

- quoted material[83]
- text strings, as in "This field may hold only the values 'M' and 'F'."
- word(s) if discussing the word(s) themselves rather than their meaning, as in "The word 'domain' has multiple meanings."
- titles of documents, articles, or publications if specified by the applicable style guide.

---

[82] This is not to be confused with ellipsis meaning omission of repeated words or phrases, as discussed in Section 2.2.6.

[83] See Section 4.3.

If quoted material includes other quoted material (or any other item enclosed in quotation marks):

- The US convention is to use double quotation marks for the outer quotation and single quotation marks for the inner quotation.
- The UK convention is to use single quotation marks for the outer quotation and double quotation marks for the inner quotation.

Do not use quotation marks for emphasis or irony, as in "This is an example of 'best practice'."

6.7.10 Obliques

An **oblique** (also known as a **solidus** or **slash**) separates alternative words. For example, one may write "he/she" instead of "he or she", while "and/or" may be used between a pair of items to indicate either or both. Thus "he/she will require a passport and/or ID card" means "he or she will require a passport, ID card or both".

Do not use an oblique to represent a singular or plural noun, as in !"column/s", which should be written as "column(s)".

6.7.11 Apostrophes

Use an apostrophe in:

- the **possessive** form of any noun phrase or name, as in "the developer's responsibility" or "Mr Lee's role"
- any contractions, such as "won't" (although these may not be acceptable)
- some names, such as "Ms O'Connell".

6.7.12 Hyphens

Use a hyphen:

- in a **compound adjective** before a modified noun (as in "low-level view", "long-term solution", "model-based design", "open-source software", and "up-to-date documentation"); some compound adjectives in **predicates** (after a verb phrase) do not require hyphens (for example, "the documentation is up to date") whereas others (such as "factory-installed" or "state-of-the-art") require hyphens in both uses.

- between a noun or adjective and a participle, as in "zero-filled" and "fast-loading"

- in numbers between "twenty-one" and "ninety-nine" (when written as words)

- in number-unit combinations used as adjectives (when the number is written using words), as in "two-second response time"; in a pair of numbers used to express a range in which the second unit is omitted, a hyphen should appear after each number, as in "a two- to three-week delay"

- in ordinal-noun combinations used as adjectives, as in "second-tier support"

- in words with certain prefixes, such as:
    - "all", as in "all-inclusive"
    - "ex" meaning "former", as in "ex-manager"
    - "pseudo", as in "pseudo-relational"
    - "self", as in "self-balancing"

- in some words (such as "meta-analysis") with a prefix ending with the same letter as the first letter of the word; others, such as "coordinate", "multipurpose", "preeminent", and "reestablish" may be hyphenated in UK usage but not in US usage

- in words starting with "re" (such as "re-sent") that might be confused with other words

- in words (such as "co-worker") that without the hyphen would look as if they should be pronounced differently
- between a prefix and a capitalized word, as in "mid-July"
- in some surnames, such as "Berners-Lee".

Do not include a hyphen between an adverb and an adjective or participle, as in *"generally-inappropriate" or *"widely-used".

6.7.13 Question and exclamation marks

Question marks have only one use in technical or business writing: to terminate each interrogative sentence.

Exclamation marks have only one use in technical or business writing, to highlight warnings in User Manuals or Standard Operating Procedures.

6.7.14 Periods, commas, and quotation marks

Most (if not all) US style guides specify that a period or comma after quoted material must appear before the closing quotation mark. Thus, one could write "The CEO has endorsed the project, stating that it will deliver 'immediate benefits.'" or "Stating that the project will deliver 'immediate benefits,' the CEO has endorsed it."

The UK convention is to punctuate quotes of complete sentences and phrases differently:

- After quoting a complete sentence, the period or comma appears before the closing quotation mark, as in "The CEO has endorsed the project, saying, 'it will deliver immediate benefits.'" or "Saying, 'it will deliver immediate benefits,' the CEO has endorsed the project."
- After quoting a phrase, the period or comma is written after the closing quotation mark (since the quoted material is not a full sentence and therefore has no period or final comma), as in "The CEO has endorsed the

project, stating that it will deliver 'immediate benefits'." or "Stating that it will deliver 'immediate benefits', the CEO has endorsed the project."

In both US and UK usage, punctuation before quoted material is as follows:

- If a full sentence is quoted after a **noun phrase** referring to the quotation, use a colon before the opening quotation mark, as in "The CEO has provided this endorsement: 'This project will deliver immediate benefits'."

- If a full sentence is quoted as the **object** of a verb such as "stated", use either a comma or "that" before the opening quotation mark, as in "The CEO has stated, 'This project will deliver immediate benefits'." or "The CEO has stated that 'this project will deliver immediate benefits'."

- If only a phrase is quoted, use no punctuation before it, as in "The CEO has stated that this project will deliver 'immediate benefits'."

If a technical document includes a character string immediately before a period or comma, that period or comma must appear after the closing quotation mark, as in "This field may hold only the values 'M' and 'F'."

The placement of a question mark before or after a closing quotation mark depends on whether a question is being quoted or the sentence containing the quotation is a question. For example, "The CIO has asked 'How long will this take?'" and "Has the CIO said 'This will take too long'?"

6.7.15 Punctuation and spaces

The rules for spaces before and after each punctuation mark are as follows:

- period (full stop), comma, colon, semicolon, question mark: no space before, one space after[84]

---

[84] There are some who prefer two spaces after a period, but the current versions of all style guides consulted specify one space.

- left parenthesis or square bracket or opening quotation mark: one space before, no space after
- right parenthesis or square bracket or closing quotation mark: no space before, one space after unless immediately followed by another punctuation mark
- dash or oblique: either:
    - no space before, no space after or
    - one space before, one space after
- apostrophe or hyphen: no space before, no space after.

6.8 Capitalization

Capitalize the first letter of the first word of each sentence unless that word is a company name or brand name that starts with a lowercase letter, such as "eBay" or "iPhone".

Do not capitalize the first letter of the first word after a colon or semicolon unless that word is "I" or a name.

6.8.1 Names

Each given name and the family name in a person's name should start with a capital letter, but any prepositions in the family name (such as "de", "von", or "van") should be in all lowercase, thus "Antoine de Saint-Exupéry", "Herbert von Karajan".

6.8.2 Headings

There are two commonly used ways to capitalize headings:

- **sentence case**, which capitalizes only the first letter of (a) the first word in the heading, and (b) any names
- **title case**, normally used for the titles of books and articles.

US rules for title case vary depending on the style guide being followed. All style guides agree that one should capitalize the first letter of the first word and each noun, verb, pronoun, adjective, and adverb. However, they have different rules for the capitalization of the first letter of the last word, the word "to", prepositions, conjunctions, and words after hyphens. Moreover, some of those rules are open to interpretation.

The UK rules for title case are simpler: capitalize the first letter of the first word and each noun, verb, pronoun, adjective, and adverb.

The Australian Government Style Manual specifies sentence case for headings.

Some style guides specify title case for top-level headings and sentence case for all other headings.

6.8.3 Specific and generic instances

It is the practice in some organizations to:

- capitalize common nouns referring to individual jurisdictions, political roles, or management positions, as in "the Government", "the President", or "the Chief Data Officer"
- not capitalize such nouns in the plural, thus "other governments", "presidents of EU member nations".

However, other organizations do not capitalize any such nouns.

When capitalizing a compound noun, the general rule is to capitalize the first letter of each word other than prepositions or articles. Thus, one would write "all Data Modelers" rather than !"all Data modelers", and "all Heads of Departments" rather than !"all Heads of departments".

It is common to make a similar distinction when referring to sections of a document, versions of a software product, and the like. Thus, a document may refer to "Section 6.1" but "the next section" and may refer to "Version 2.3" but "the latest version".

6.8.4 Other capitalization rules

It is typical to capitalize the names of:

- key technology components (such as "Data Vault", "Star Schema", and "Operational Data Store")
- individual modeling artifacts such as entity classes, attributes, and subject areas.

Chapter 7. Common errors

This chapter covers some of the errors in documents I have reviewed over the past decades.

7.1 Ambiguity

There are many ways to make a sentence ambiguous (able to be interpreted in more than one way), including (a) careless use of **pronouns**, (b) **prepositional phrases** that may apply to more than one **noun phrase**, and (c) words and phrases with multiple meanings,.

7.1.1 Pronouns

A **pronoun** may be ambiguous if there is more than one **noun phrase** to which the pronoun can refer. For example:

- In !"The developer told the test manager that she was not responsible for the outcome." the pronoun "she" might refer to the developer or the test manager.
- In !"Despite differences of opinion between the Data Modeler and the Database Administrator, he eventually acquiesced to the enforcement of all constraints after each load." the pronoun "he" might refer to the Data Modeler or the Database Administrator.

Such ambiguity can be removed by:

- following the pronoun by the appropriate noun phrase in parentheses.
- replacing the pronoun by "the latter" or "the former"
- replacing the pronoun by the appropriate noun phrase (not always appropriate).

The following revised sentences illustrate two such edits:

- "The developer told the test manager that she (the developer) was not responsible for the outcome."
- "Despite differences of opinion between the Data Modeler and the Database Administrator, the latter eventually acquiesced to the enforcement of all constraints after each load."

7.1.2 Prepositional phrases that may apply to more than one noun phrase

A prepositional phrase can apply to more than one noun phrase in the same sentence. For example:

- !"There have been requests for this restriction to be removed from both the New York and London offices." may mean either (a) the requests have come from those offices, or (b) the requests have been for removal of restrictions from those offices.

If the first interpretation is intended, moving the prepositional phrase makes this clear, as in "There have been requests from both the New York and London offices for this restriction to be removed." If the second interpretation is intended, the sentence needs to be recast, as in "We have been requested to remove this restriction from both the New York and London offices."

7.1.3 Words and phrases with multiple meanings

Ambiguity can result from the use of a word or phrase with multiple meanings. For example, "sanction" means "allow" (as in "this syntax is sanctioned by the standard") or "disallow" (in line with the meaning of the noun "sanction").

7.1.4 Syntactic ambiguity

There are phrases or clauses that can be interpreted in more than one way. For example:

- "more experienced candidates" may mean "more candidates who are experienced" or "candidates who are more experienced"
- !"We do not know how motivated team members are to spend time working on this." may mean "we do not know how those team members who are motivated will spend time" or "we do not know how much motivation there is for team members to spend time".

Sometimes, a phrase or clause that can be interpreted in more than one way is followed by text which only allows for one interpretation. Meanwhile, the reader has had to juggle alternative interpretations, consciously or unconsciously. For example:

- Until the reader reaches the end of the second sentence in "Businesses that had paid their staff more had kept them. Those that had not faced the challenge of finding more staff." the words after "Those" to in the second sentence could be read as a relative clause, leading the reader to expect another clause, as in "Those that had not faced the challenge of finding more staff continued to pay their existing staff at the previous rates."
- The use of "before" instead of "beforehand" may lead to more than one initial interpretation. In a sentence starting "Three years before we upgraded to version 10, ..." it is not immediately clear whether we are about to find out what happened three years before the upgrade or what happened after the upgrade three years ago.

7.1.5 Temporal ambiguity

Section 3.9.8.3 discusses how phrases such as "later this year", "in the new year", or "at the end of the month" are ambiguous. This is because such phrases require the reader to refer to the document's publication date (and any revision dates) to try to establish which year, month, or week the phrase refers to. Therefore, in any permanent document, use specific years, months, and (if necessary) days rather than phrases such as these. For example, "A new version of this software is to be released in early 2019." rather than !"A new version of this software is to be released early in the new year."

A sentence that includes a temporal phrase and refers to more than one event may be ambiguous. For example, the sentence "Please advise when we can upgrade the system in September." could be interpreted as (a) wanting a reply in September, or (b) wanting to upgrade the system in September.

The term "biweekly" may mean either every other week or twice a week, so use "every other week" or "twice weekly" (as appropriate) instead of "biweekly". Similarly, use "every other month" or "twice monthly" instead of "bimonthly", and "every other year" or "twice yearly" instead of "biannual" or "biennial".

7.1.6   Other sources of ambiguity

There are other ways in which a sentence may be ambiguous:

- The sentence !"Uniqueness constraints may govern one column or multiple columns." looks straightforward enough but it is not clear that a single constraint may govern more than one column. It may be that, while the set of constraints may between them govern more than one column, each individual constraint may only govern one column. This ambiguity can be removed by rephrasing the sentence as "Each uniqueness constraint may govern one or more columns."

- In meeting minutes which included the sentence !"The project manager agreed to finish the project.", it was not clear whether the project manager had (a) agreed to shut down the project prematurely, or (b) agreed to continuing the project until complete.

- In advice that a stakeholder to be interviewed "will arrive late on Friday", it was not clear whether (a) that person would arrive after their scheduled start time or (b) sometime late in the afternoon or evening.

- In a report that referred to "more complex questions", it was not clear whether these were (a) questions that were more complex than existing questions, or (b) further complex questions in addition to the existing complex questions.

7.2 Word order

Errors in the order of words in a sentence may require the reader to put in more effort to understand the sentence and may cause ambiguity or misinterpretation.

7.2.1 Dangling modifiers

A **dangling modifier** is a phrase at the start of a sentence which qualifies something other than the **subject** of that sentence. For example:

- Rephrase !"As the database administrator, all tables must have a primary key." as "As the database administrator, I require that all tables have a primary key."

- Rephrase !"Formerly the CEO, we discussed the options with Mr Smith." as "We discussed the options with Mr Smith, formerly the CEO."

- Rephrase !"Being the largest table, we believe that priority should be given to deleting out of date rows." as "As this is the largest table, we believe that priority should be given to deleting out of date rows."

- Rephrase !"At a transaction rate of more than 1,000 per second, we recommend a more powerful server be used." as "Given the transaction rate of more than 1,000 per second, we recommend a more powerful server be used."

- Rephrase !"Like other projects, we have reported regularly." as "As in other projects, we have reported regularly."

- Rephrase !"Having passed all tests, the Test Manager authorized the release of Version 11.5 to the User Acceptance environment." as "Version 11.5 having passed all tests, the Test Manager authorized its release to the User Acceptance environment." or "As it had passed all tests, the Test Manager authorized the release of Version 11.5 to the User Acceptance environment."

7.2.2 Misplaced modifiers

A **misplaced modifier** is a phrase that is not next to the **noun phrase** it modifies. This often results in ambiguity, although in many cases, only one interpretation is plausible so the reader can interpret the sentence with minimal effort:

- Consider !"The same sample model was loaded into each candidate software product provided by the Department." Since the Department provided the sample model rather than the software products, rephrase this as "The same sample model provided by the Department was loaded into each candidate software product."

- Consider !"A new version of this software is to be released by the vendor with the remaining required functionality in the new year." Obviously, the new version (rather than the vendor) will include the functionality but rephrasing this sentence as "A new version of this software, with the remaining required functionality, is to be released in 2019." would have made it easier for the reader to infer that relationship.

- Rephrase !"You should contact the Department before you arrive by email." as "You should contact the Department by email before you arrive."

- Rephrase !"Meals will be provided to all team members packaged in disposable containers." as "Meals packaged in disposable containers will be provided to all team members."

- Rephrase !"We will start work on all enhancements included in the latest round of change requests but too complex to implement in this release due to insufficient time and resources in 2020." as "In 2020 we will start work on all enhancements (a) included in the latest round of change requests, but (b) too complex to implement in the next release due to insufficient time and resources." It might be preferable to split this sentence, as "A number of enhancements included in the latest round of change requests were too complex to implement in this release due to insufficient time and resources. We will start work on those enhancements in 2020."

Some sentences may be less easy to disambiguate:

- !"It was later established that the modifications included were inappropriate by Mr. Smith." may be interpreted as either:
    - "It was later established by Mr. Smith that the modifications included were inappropriate." or
    - "It was later established that the modifications included by Mr. Smith were inappropriate."
- !"The failure to back up the data was described as an inexcusable error by the database administrator." may be interpreted as either:
    - "The database administrator's failure to back up the data was described as an inexcusable error." or
    - "The database administrator described the failure to back up the data as an inexcusable error."
- Consider !"They were among the people facing retrenchment by managers who were promoted last week." Who was promoted? The people facing retrenchment or the managers?
- Consider !"We've taken steps to avoid what happened for the last few years." Were the steps taken over the last few years, or did whatever happen occur over the last few years?

7.2.3 Separation of related phrases

In *The Complete Plain Words*, Gowers wrote: "do not ... strain your reader's memory by widely separating parts of a sentence that are closely related to one another." An example of such separation is:

- !"We sent those stakeholders who had provided feedback after attending the requirements gathering sessions for this project the updated requirements specification." This is a sentence with two objects, the indirect object "stakeholders" and the direct object "requirements specification", that are too far apart. This sentence should be rephrased "We sent the updated requirements specification to those stakeholders who had provided feedback after attending the requirements gathering sessions for this project."

7.2.4 Subject-verb reversal in indirect questions

An error that occurs occasionally is reversal of the **subject** and **verb** in an **indirect question** (reflecting the word order in the direct question). For example, *"We enquired why is this happening." should be rephrased "We enquired why this is happening."

7.3 Confusing singular and plural

Phrases starting with "type of" or "kind of" are often written preceded by "these" or "those", as in *"these type of tools". This is nonstandard: use "this type" or "these types".

A common error is to make the verb agree with the last noun in a complex noun phrase, as in *"This set of enhancements are included in the next release."

The following sentences exhibit similar errors:

- *"The workload – over 100 updates – are taking longer than expected."
- *"Ignoring these issues have led to deteriorating data quality."
- *"Each of the operators have received training."
- *"A set of constraints have been added."
- *"A range of options are available."

The words "number of" before a noun may take either a **singular** or **plural** verb. "A number of defects are now fixed." and "The number of defects is normally more." are both correct: "a number of" is an alternative for "many", which takes a plural verb, while "the number of" refers to a singular concept.

7.4 Plural noun phrases

The use of a plural subject may often result in ambiguity. For example, !"All foreign keys must point to an existing row in the other table." could be interpreted as meaning that all foreign keys should point to the same row. It should be rephrased "Each foreign key must point to an existing row in the other table."

To avoid the possibility of ambiguity, it is good practice to write each statement with a singular subject if possible:

- Statements of rules:
    - Rephrase !"Tables must have a surrogate key as the primary key." as "Each table must have a surrogate key as the primary key."
    - Rephrase !"Business keys should never be used as the primary key of any table." as "A business key should never be used as the primary key of any table."
- Statements of definitions: Rephrase !"Business keys are the attribute or combination of attributes that uniquely identify an instance of a business entity." as "A business key is the attribute or combination of attributes that uniquely identifies an instance of a business entity."
- Observations: Rephrase !"These tables do not have a business key." as "None of these tables has a business key."

The use of a plural object may compromise the intended message. For example, !"Separate the terms in a name with an underscore." should be rephrased "Separate each consecutive pair of terms in each name with an underscore."

7.5 Misuse of determiners

The definite article "the" is often misused: it is only correct before a singular noun when referring to:

- the only instance of that concept that exists, as in "the Earth"
- the only instance of that concept that exists in the context already established, as in "the CEO" (in an organization)
- (where an instance of the concept has already been referred to) the instance already referred to (by inclusion of "same" after "the"), as in "the same day"

- (where two instances of the concept exist—or exist in the context already established—and one has already been referred to) the other instance (by inclusion of "other" after "the"), as in "the other issue"
- the only instance of that concept that meets the criterion or criteria specified:
    - by one or more attributive adjectives or nouns between "the" and the noun, as in "the latest release", "the database server"
    - in a qualifying clause after the noun, as in "the person named in the application"
    - in both a qualifying clause and one or more attributive adjectives or nouns between "the" and the noun, as in "the destination city specified in the flight booking request".

Similarly, "the" is only correct before a plural noun when referring to:

- all instances of a concept, as in "the Australian states"
- all instances of a concept that exist in the context already established, as in "the members" (of a team)
- (if particular instances of the concept have already been referred to) the instances already referred to (by inclusion of "same" after "the"), as in "the same products"
- (if particular instances of the concept have already been referred to) all other instances (by inclusion of "other" after "the"), as in "the other rooms"
- the only instances of that concept that meet the criterion or criteria specified:
    - by one or more attributive adjectives or nouns between "the" and the noun, as in "the updated records", "the Sydney offices"
    - in a qualifying clause after the noun, as in "the passengers specified in the booking"
    - in both a qualifying clause and one or more attributive adjectives or nouns between "the" and the noun, as in "the urgent orders placed by the customer".

Use of an indefinite article ("a" or "an") instead of "each" may obscure the meaning of a sentence. For example, it is not clear whether the clause !"since a table contains data sourced from a single source system" refers to a single table or to every table. This clause should therefore be rephrased "since each table contains data sourced from a single source system".

The determiners "less" and "fewer" are often misused; Section 6.2.5 sets out the rules for their use.

7.6   Incomplete sentences

A clause containing only a **nonfinite verb phrase**—such as *"The highlight being the completion of the Customer Management project."—or starting with a **subordinating conjunction**—such as *"Although this failed to materialize"—is not a complete sentence.

7.7   Confusing objects and their names

It is important to make a distinction between objects and their names. The sentence !"The primary key is the table name followed by _KEY." does not make sense; it should be rephrased "The name of each primary key is the table name followed by '_KEY'."

7.8   Imprecise terminology

Most technical and business communities have developed terminology with precise meanings. For example, in the data community, there is a consensus that:

- business concepts and the artifacts created to represent them (entity or object classes) have attributes, whereas
- tables in a relational or object-relational database have columns (rather than fields or attributes) and rows (rather than records).

Despite this consensus, it is all too common to find references to attributes, fields, or records in a table.

Another common error is the use of the term "database" to refer to a database management system. A database is a collection of data that is stored within a database management system.

Use consistent terminology. For example, the sentence !"Only use abbreviations from the List of Allowable Abbreviations, or if the term does not yet have an allowable abbreviation, create an appropriate abbreviation and add it to the master list." uses two different terms for what is presumably the same list.

Writers of documentation for organizations operating in a particular industry should familiarize themselves with the meanings of terms used in that industry. For example, in the rail transport industry, the terms "train" and "locomotive" have distinct meanings but are often used wrongly.

7.9 Term overload

Some terms may be **overloaded**, not by giving them different meanings but by using them in related but different contexts. The most common term to be overloaded is "primary key": I have often encountered, in a single document, statements that each table has one primary key as well as statements that each row has a primary key. Since most tables have more than one row, such statements contradict each other. One may avoid this by using the term "primary key definition" to refer to the table property and reserve "primary key" for the unique value (or concatenation of values) in each row of a table.

7.10 Incorrect prepositions

A common error is the use of an incorrect preposition after a noun or verb, such as *"compliance of" or *"complying to". If you are unsure about the correct preposition to use, Section 6.2.7 provides some advice.

Another common error is to use "to" after "between", as in *"between two to four". This should be "between two and four" or "from two to four".

7.11 Confusing adjectives and adverbs

Most words ending in '-ly' are adverbs, but there are also adjectives ending in '-ly', such as "costly", "early", "likely", and "timely". Some writers treat these as if they were adverbs. For example, *"This was completed timely."

7.12 Breaking chronological order

I occasionally encounter statements such as !"the project team has completed implementation and design". Design precedes implementation in the normal sequence of events, so should precede it in any sentence that refers to both.

7.13 Using the wrong conjunction

7.13.1 At the start of a relative clause

Do not introduce a **restrictive relative clause** (one that modifies the scope of the preceding noun phrase) with "which", as in *"these are the modules which have been updated". Use "that" instead, thus "these are the modules that have been updated".

Do not introduce a **nonrestrictive relative clause** (one that only provides more information about a noun phrase) with "that", as in *"we have updated these modules, that were included in the latest release". Use "which" instead, thus "we have updated these modules, which were included in the latest release".

7.13.2   In a series

A common error is to use "and" rather than "or" (or vice versa) in a series:

- "The system must be available day or night." should read "The system must be available day and night."
- "Entry of negative and fractional values will generate an error message." should read "Entry of a negative or fractional value will generate an error message."

7.14   Errors in usage

This section lists common ways in which words and phrases are wrongly used.

7.14.1   Commonly confused words, abbreviations, and phrases

Where two or more words have the same or similar pronunciation, writers may inadvertently use the wrong word. I have encountered "reign in" rather than "rein in" and "wave fees" rather than "waive fees". Among other words that may be confused are:

accept/except	affect/effect	allusion/illusion
allude/elude	amend/emend	bare/bear
break/brake	canvas/canvass	capital/Capitol
commiserate/commensurate	complement/compliment	confidant/confident
copyrighter/copywriter	co-respondent/correspondent	council/counsel
desperate/disparate	discreet/discrete	elicit/illicit
flare/flair	forward/foreword	hypercritical/hypocritical
incidents/incidence	instance/instants	intensional/intentional
its/it's	lightening/lightning	loath/loathe
ordnance/ordinance	passed/past	precede/proceed
principle/principal	role/roll	sheer/shear
sight/site/cite	sort/sought	stationary/stationery
there/their/they're	to/too/two	uncharted/unchartered

The following words are also sometimes confused:

- "among": three or more; "between": two only
- "denormalized": previously normalized but no longer normalized; "unnormalized": never normalized
- "function": purpose; "functionality": effectiveness in fulfilling purpose
- "historic": famous; "historical": to do with history
- "especially": particularly, more than usually; "specially": for a special purpose, in a special manner, specifically
- "graphical": visual, in the form of a graphic; "graphic" (adjective): explicit, vivid; "graphic" (noun): visual representation.

Other words and abbreviations that may be confused include:

appraise/apprise	assume/presume	averse/adverse
breach/broach	corroborate/collaborate	elemental/elementary
exception/exemption	farther/further	flaunt/flout
farther/further	i.e./e.g.	imminent/eminent/immanent
infer/imply	interstate/intrastate	lend/borrow/loan
lie/lay	loose/lose	misinformation/disinformation
prescribe/proscribe	quiet/quite	regretfully/regrettably
specialty/speciality	systemic/systematic	then/than
underlying/underline	uninterested/disinterested	variance/variation

The word "last" is often used when "previous" is meant. For example, while "the last time this program was run" is appropriate when referring to the final occasion when it was run, it is inappropriate when referring to the latest occasion prior to the date of the communication.

A common error made by some IT professionals is to wrongly use the term "relation" when intending to refer to a "relationship". The term "relation" has a specific meaning in set theory which is the basis of the relational model of data proposed by Edward F. Codd in 1970. A "relationship", by contrast, is an association between two or more entity classes in an Entity–Relationship Model (a common data modeling technique proposed by Peter Chen in 1976).

The terms "First Name" and "Last Name" are often used to refer to a person's given and family names. However, there are many cultures in which the family name precedes the given names. Use "Given Name" and "Family Name" instead.

To state that something now takes a third of the time it took previously, "three times as fast" is preferable to "three times faster". However, it is unlikely that the difference is exact, so "approximately three times as fast" would be preferable.

7.14.2 Similar but distinct phrases

Similar words and phrases are sometimes confused:

- The word "because" is a **conjunction**, whereas "because of" is a **preposition**. We may write "Because data can be lost, integrity checks must be run." or "Because of data loss, integrity checks must be run."

- The **adverb** "altogether" means "wholly" or "totally", as in "altogether different". The phrase "all together" means "in the same place" or "at the same time", as in "This was the first occasion on which stakeholders were all together." The phrase "all together" may be split, thus we could rewrite the last clause as "This was the first occasion on which all stakeholders were together."

- The **preposition** "in case of" is used before a noun phrase defining a possible future event against which precautions should be taken, as in "In case of data loss, run a backup first." The preposition "In the case of" means "regarding", as in "In the case of the lost data, no decision has yet been made." "In case of" is often wrongly used instead of "in the event of" to mean "requiring action when it happens", as in !"In case of data loss, retrieve from the last backup."

- The **adjective** "everyday" means "normal", "ordinary", "routine", or "common", as in "This is an everyday occurrence." The **noun phrase** "every day" is an adverb of frequency in clauses such as "The database is backed up every day."

- The **determiner** "few" used alone means "not many" or "insufficient", as in "There are few things that could be done to improve this situation." By contrast, "a few" means "more than one", as in "There are a few things that could be done to improve this situation."

- The **adverb** "maybe" means "perhaps" or "possibly", as in "maybe we will need to adopt a different approach". The **verb phrase** "may be" means "is possibly" or "are possibly", as in "this may be the best approach", or "will possibly be", as in "we may be forced to adopt a different approach".

- The **noun** "meantime" requires "in the" beforehand, whereas the **adverb** "meanwhile" does not require "in the" beforehand.

- The words "the most" before an **adjective** imply the best in some measure, as in "This is the most effective solution." By contrast, "a most" means merely "very", as in "This is a most effective solution."

- The **preposition** "onto" means "to a position on", as in "we are migrating this application onto the new database platform". The phrase "on to" only occurs when a phrasal verb ending in "on" has as its object something to which movement occurs, as in "this week we move on to the next set of enhancements".

- The **conjunctions** "though" and "although" are synonymous: "Although this is a common approach, it is inappropriate in this situation." and "Though this is a common approach, it is inappropriate in this situation." have the same meaning. However, "though" (but not "although") may also be used as an **adverb**, meaning "however", as in "This approach, though, is inappropriate."

7.14.3 Plurals often used wrongly

The plural nouns "criteria" and "phenomena" are often used as if they were singular. For example, *"this is the only mandatory criteria" should be rephrased "this is the only mandatory criterion", and *"this is a common phenomena" should be rephrased "this is a common phenomenon".

7.14.4 Words, phrases, and clauses often used wrongly

The verb forms *"comprises of" and *"is comprised of" are nonstandard. Use "consists of" or "is composed of" to list the components of something.

The verb "comprise" is listed in many dictionaries with both the "be composed of" and "compose" meanings, as in !"This training module comprises online course material and a workbook." and !"Online course material and a workbook comprise this training module." For this reason, do not use "comprise" anywhere. Thus, !"The primary key comprises the combination of the foreign key and the timestamp." should be rephrased "The primary key consists of the combination of the foreign key and the timestamp."

A common error is to use **"beg the question"**—a valid clause, with the meanings "cause someone to ask the question" and "ignore the question on the basis that it has already been answered"—to mean "raise the question". For example, !"This begs the question of how we can recover from this loss." should be rephrased "This raises the question of how we can recover from this loss."

When using the past continuous verb form, the correct forms are **"used to"** in a positive assertion, as in "This used to be the only option." and **"use to"** in a negative assertion or a question, as in "This did not use to be the only option." or "Did this use to be the only option?" It is incorrect to write "use to" in a positive assertion (as in *"This use to be the only option.") or "used to" in a negative assertion or a question, as in *"This did not used to be the only option." or *"Did this used to be the only option?"

The verb **"try"** may be followed by an **infinitive** verb, as in "try to complete". Many consider the alternative form **"try and complete"** to nonstandard.

The following phrases and clauses are nonstandard; presumably they result from mishearing valid phrases and clauses:

- "jump into conclusions" rather than "jumping to conclusions"
- "tow the line" rather than "toe the line"
- "would of" rather than "would have", etc.
- "unchartered territory" rather than "uncharted territory"
- "daylight savings" rather than "daylight saving".

7.14.5 Common misspellings

The following are misspellings of valid words:

- *"byeproduct" should be "byproduct"
- *"disfunctional" should be "dysfunctional"
- *"definate" should be "definite"

- *"intergrated" should be "integrated"
- *"seperate" should be "separate"
- *"supercede" should be "supersede".

7.14.6 Nonexistent words

The following words and phrases are nonstandard:

- *"agreeance" rather than "agreement"
- *"alot" rather than "a lot" or "allot"
- *"infact" rather than "in fact"
- *"inside of" rather than "inside"
- *"irregardless" rather than "regardless"
- *"supposably" rather than "supposedly"
- *"theirselves" rather than "themselves".

7.14.7 Confusion between plural and possessive

Plurals never have apostrophes whereas possessives (except "its") always have apostrophes. Thus *"team member's review each others work" should be "Team members review each other's work".

7.15 Verbosity

7.15.1 Superfluous words

Some expressions use more words than necessary. For example:

- "added bonus": drop "added"
- "and also": drop "also"
- "emergency situation": drop "situation"
- "future prospects": drop "future"

- "whether or not": drop "or not"
- "9am in the morning": drop "in the morning".

If a list of items starts with "such as" or "for example", adding "etc." or "and so on" at the end of the list is unnecessary.

Writers sometimes include **adjectives** that add little (if anything) to a sentence's meaning. For example, "a modern up-to-date data platform" does not need both "modern" and "up-to-date".

While some **adverbs** may supply essential additional information, some (such as "very") may often be removed without altering sentence meaning.

A common practice by writers who have previously worked as programmers is to follow an "if" clause by "then", as in "If the information is not available, then it can be left blank". In sentences like these, "then" may be dropped.

7.15.2 Repetition

In the sentences !"These need to be stored in the data warehouse tables, using the same column names as in the source system. They need to be stored in the data warehouse tables because they are important for a business understanding of the data." the second sentence repeats much of the first sentence.

Rephrasing this as "These need to be stored in the data warehouse tables, using the same column names as in the source system. This is because they are important for a business understanding of the data." saves eight words.

7.15.3 Unwieldy sentences

Here are just two examples of sentences that may be rewritten to be shorter and clearer:

- !"Taking into consideration the requirements of the Department, the identification of which was the objective of the workshops conducted as part of this project, and the capabilities and functionality of the software products which were included in the shortlist agreed with the Department, evaluation of those products against those requirements was conducted, the results of which form the content of this report, it being a contractual deliverable."

  may be rewritten as

  "This report, as required by the contract, (a) summarizes the Department's requirements (identified in the workshops conducted as part of this project), and (b) evaluates each of the shortlisted software products against those requirements."

- !"For those functions which are listed in the Requirements Specification for this project and for which successful execution was unable to be achieved, the support service provided by the shortlisted vendor was contacted, leading to either advice from the vendor as to how to achieve successful execution or to advice that the function would form part of a subsequent release or would not."

  may be rewritten as

  "For each required function which could not be executed successfully, the project team contacted the vendor's support service. In each case, the vendor replied with either (a) instructions for executing the function or (b) a statement of whether the function would form part of a subsequent release."

7.16   Punctuation errors

The most common punctuation errors occur with commas, perhaps because of their many functions:

- A comma after a long **subject noun phrase**, as in *"The second phase of the project, will start in 2023." is incorrect unless it is one of a pair of commas used to set off a parenthetical, as in "The second phase of the project, the retirement of the current system, will start in 2023."

- Failure to include both opening and closing parenthetical commas, as in *"The retirement of the current system, which will take two months will start in 2023.", is incorrect.

- A **comma splice** is the use of a comma to separate two **independent clauses** without an intervening **conjunction**, as in *"Yesterday's data has been loaded, it is available to users."

- A **run-on sentence** includes more than one **independent clause** without any intervening conjunction or punctuation, as in *"Yesterday's data has been loaded it is available to users." Rewrite this as:
    - "Yesterday's data has been loaded. It is available to users."
    - "Yesterday's data has been loaded; it is available to users." or
    - "Yesterday's data has been loaded and is available to users."

Part 2: Reference material

Chapter 8. Differences between US and UK Standard English

There are more similarities than differences between US and UK written English. However, it is useful to be aware of the differences in vocabulary, spelling, phrasing, and punctuation. UK English is the norm in Australia, New Zealand, South Africa, and other British Commonwealth countries, although Canada uses a mix of US and UK conventions. Ireland also uses UK English, as does the European Union alongside its other official languages.

8.1 Vocabulary

Some terms have different meanings in US and UK English. For example:

- "alternate" means both "other" and "every other" in US English; UK English uses "alternative" to mean "other" and "alternate" to mean only "every other"
- "concession" means "lease of premises for a particular use" in US English, but "price reduction for a category of person" in UK English
- "first floor" means "ground level" in US English, but "floor above ground level" in UK English
- "solicitor" in US English means "door-to-door salesman", but "legal representative" in UK English
- to "table" a matter in US English means "delay discussion of it", but "suggest it for discussion" in UK English
- "thru" in US English means "until", whereas "through" in UK English means "during" or "across".

Table 10 lists some concepts for which US and UK English have different terms.

US term	UK term	US term	UK term	US term	UK term
airplane	aeroplane	expiration	expiry	period	full stop
cellphone	mobile phone	expressway	motorway	toward	towards
check mark	tick	fall	autumn	vacation	holiday
counterclockwise	anticlockwise	mailbox	postbox	zip code	postcode
elevator	lift				

Table 10: US and UK terms

Specific industries (such as rail transport and the auto industry) have industry-specific vocabularies, including concepts for which US and UK English use different terms. These are outside the scope of this book.

8.2 Spelling

Table 11 lists some words that are spelled differently in US and UK English.

US spelling	UK spelling	US spelling	UK spelling	US spelling	UK spelling
aluminum	aluminium	defense	defence	mold	mould
artifact	artefact	dialog	dialogue	skeptic	sceptic
catalog	catalogue	gray	grey	thru	through

Table 11: US and UK spelling

There are other differences in US and UK spelling:

- In both US and UK usage "adviser" is more common, but "advisor" is an alternative used more in the US than the UK.

- UK usage spells the past tense forms of "burn" as either "burned" or "burnt", whereas US usage prefers "burned", reserving "burnt" for the associated adjective.

- In UK usage, a "check" is an examination of something whereas a "cheque" is a means of payment. US usage spells both as "check".

- In US usage, "inquire" and "inquiry" are more common in both official and informal contexts. In UK usage, "inquire" and "inquiry" are used in official contexts, and "enquire" and "enquiry" in informal contexts.

- In UK usage, "forward" and "onward" are adjectives, whereas "forwards" and "onwards" are adverbs. In US usage "forward" and "onward" are used as both adjectives and adverbs.

- In UK usage, "geographical" is preferred, while "geographic" is preferred in US usage.

- In UK usage, "licence" is a noun whereas "license" is a verb. US usage spells both as "license".

- In UK usage, "practice" is a noun whereas "practise" is a verb. US usage spells both as "practice".

- In UK usage, a "program" is application code whereas a "programme" is a set of activities or performances. US usage spells both as "program".

- In UK usage, a "story" is a narrative whereas a "storey" is a floor of a building. US usage spells both as "story".

- In UK usage, a "tyre" is fitted to a wheel whereas "tire" means "fatigue" or "become fatigued". US usage spells both as "tire".

- UK usage accepts both "while" and "whilst" as conjunctions, whereas US usage prefers "while".

There are also differences in word endings:

- Words ending with '-er' in US usage (such as "center") end with '-re' in UK usage ("centre" in this case). Words spelled using '-er' in both usages include "alter", "chapter", "character", "diameter", "disaster", "enter", "filter", "interpreter", "letter", "member", "number", "parameter", "perimeter", "proper", and "tender", as well as month names ending in '-ber'. Words spelled using '-re' in both usages include "acre" and "mediocre". The spelling "meter" is used for a device in both usages and for the measurement unit in US usage (for which the UK spelling is "metre").

- Many words ending with '-or' in US usage (such as "**color**") end with '-our' in UK usage ("**colour**" in this case).

- While the US usage prefers '-ize' and '-yze' endings, UK usage prefers '-ise' and '-yse'. Similarly, the '-ization', '-ized', '-izes', '-izing', '-yzed', '-yzes', and '-yzing' endings in US usage may be written as '-isation', '-ised', '-ises', '-ising', '-ysed', '-yses', and '-ysing' respectively in UK usage. Within a document or set of documents following UK conventions, usage should be consistent. Words spelled using '-ise' in both usages include "**advertise**", "**advise**", "**appraise**", "**apprise**", "**clockwise**", "**comprise**", "**compromise**", "**concise**", "**devise**", "**enterprise**", "**exercise**", "**expertise**", "**franchise**", "**improvise**", "**likewise**", "**merchandise**", "**otherwise**", "**precise**", "**premise**", "**promise**", "**revise**", "**supervise**", "**surprise**", "**televise**", and "**wise**". Words spelled using '-ize' in both usages include "**size**".

- Words ending with '-dgment' in US usage (such as "**acknowledgment**" and "**judgment**") end with '-dgement' in UK usage.

- There is variation between US and UK usage with respect to doubling a final letter when adding a suffix. For example:
  - US usage prefers "**modeling**", "**modeled**", and "**modeler**" whereas UK usage prefers "**modelling**", "**modelled**", and "**modeller**".
  - US usage prefers "**canceled**" and "**cancelation**" whereas UK usage prefers "**cancelled**" and "**cancellation**".
  - US usage prefers "**install**" and "**installment**" whereas UK usage prefers "**instal**" and "**instalment**".
  - US usage prefers "**enroll**" and "**enrollment**" whereas UK usage prefers "**enrol**" and "**enrolment**".

- In general, US usage prefers "**spelled**" while UK usage prefers "**spelt**".

8.3 Phrases

US and UK English differ in the way certain phrases are written. For example:

- In numbers written in words, UK usage includes "**and**" after "**hundred**", as in "**one hundred and ten**", whereas US usage omits "**and**", thus "**one hundred ten**". Similarly, UK usage includes "**and**" after "**thousand**", "million", "billion", and so on, as in "one thousand and thirty" (UK) and "one thousand thirty" (US).

- US usage prefers "different than". This is not generally accepted in UK usage, which prefers "different from" or "different to".

8.4   Dates

In US usage the month number or name precedes the day number, as in "July 4, 2001" (with a comma), whereas in UK usage the month number or name follows the day number, as in "4 July 2001" (without a comma). For this reason, do not use all-numeral dates such as !"7/4/2001", as these are ambiguous due to the different conventions.

8.5   Punctuation

US and UK punctuation conventions differ as follows:

- After a person's abbreviated title:
    - the US convention is to always add a period, thus "Mr.", "Prof."
    - the UK convention is to add a full stop only if the last letter of the abbreviation is different to that of the full form, thus "Mr", "Prof."
- After "e.g." or "i.e.", the US convention is to always add a comma, whereas the UK convention adds no comma.
- When a quoted passage includes a quotation:
    - the US convention is to use double quotation marks for the outer quotation and single quotation marks for the inner quotation
    - the UK convention is to use single quotation marks for the outer quotation and double quotation marks for the inner quotation.
- There are differences between US and UK conventions for placement of periods and commas at the end of a quotation, covered in Section 6.7.14.

- When writing a time of day, the US convention is to write a colon between the hours and minutes, whereas a full stop (period) is an alternative allowed by some UK style guides.
- While US and UK hyphenation conventions are mostly the same, some words hyphenated in a UK publication would not be hyphenated in a US publication.

8.6 Personal Names

Personal names include the middle initial in US usage; this is rare in UK usage.

8.7 Title case

US rules for title case vary depending on the style guide being followed. All style guides agree that one should capitalize the first letter of the first word and each noun, verb, pronoun, adjective, and adverb. However, they have different rules for the capitalization of the first letter of the last word, the word "to", prepositions, conjunctions, and words after hyphens. Moreover, some of those rules are open to interpretation.

The UK rules for title case are simpler: capitalize the first letter of the first word and each noun, verb, pronoun, adjective, and adverb.

Chapter 9. The building blocks of English

This chapter provides more detail about the various word classes, including how words in each class **inflect** (change in different contexts), as well as a guide to the construction of each type of phrase.

A word class is best defined in terms of the behavior of its members, either:

1. the classes of other words which class members may precede or follow — for example, an **article** ("a", "an", or "the") may precede a **noun** but not a **verb**; or
2. the changes that occur to class members in certain contexts.

Using the first technique alone would inevitably require circular definitions. Fortunately, the **noun** and **verb** classes exhibit unique inflections in English.

Of course, if the class contains few words, it is possible to list those words. This is the case with the **articles**: "a", "an" and "the".

9.1   Nouns

A **noun** is a word (or sequence of words) that signifies one or more instances of a person, organization, place, or concrete or abstract thing (such as an event, arrangement, or quality), such as "author", "government department", "country", "building", "payment", "contract", and "weight". These examples are all **common nouns**; if we want to refer to an individual person, organization, ethnic group, nationality, place, language, month, day, publication, brand, or product, we use a **proper noun**[85].

---

[85] Defined in Section 9.1.5.

A more rigorous definition is that in English we can add a **possessive suffix** to the noun signifying a concept to associate it with one of its assets, characteristics, or circumstances, as in "team's achievements". All nouns exhibit this behavior; the only words to do so other than nouns are some **indefinite pronouns**[86] (as in "everyone's responsibility").

9.1.1   Possessives

For **singular nouns**, or plural nouns not ending in '-s', the possessive suffix is an apostrophe followed by 's'[87], as in "manager's decision" or "women's team". For plural nouns ending in '-s', the suffix is an apostrophe without the following 's' (as in "passengers' bags").

9.1.2   Compound nouns

Compound nouns consist of two or more words which together behave as a noun. The individual words may be separated by a space, as in "business rule", or by a hyphen, as in "take-off".[88]

A compound noun may be formed from:

- multiple nouns (such as "data warehouse", "data modeling"[89]), using spaces

---

[86] Defined in Section 9.4.

[87] Not to be confused with the use of an apostrophe before 's' to represent "is" in "it's", "how's", "who's", "when's" or "where's", or "us" as in "let's".

[88] Strictly speaking single-word nouns formed from two or more words, such as "database" or "warehouse", are also compound nouns.

[89] The word "modeling" is an example of a noun formed from a verb; such nouns are known as **gerunds** (defined in Section 9.1.3).

- one or more nouns preceded by one or more **adjectives** (such as "relational database", "foreign key", "Chief Executive Officer", "operating model"[90]), using spaces

- one or more nouns preceded by a **compound adjective** (consisting of an adjective and noun), in which case the compound adjective must use a hyphen (such as "cutting-edge technology") and be separated from the noun by a space

- a noun followed by an adjective (such as "Attorney General", "Governor-General"), using a space or a hyphen

- two or more nouns separated by **prepositions** (such as "Chief of Staff"), using spaces

- a **phrasal verb**[91] acting as a noun (such as "wrap-up", "take-off"), using a hyphen (or written as a single word)

- a noun preceded by an **adverb**[92] (such as "up train"), using spaces.

The plural form of a compound noun is generated in one of two ways:

- for a noun followed by an adjective, or two nouns separated by a preposition, form the plural of the first or only noun, such as "Attorneys General", "Chiefs of Staff"),

- in all other cases, form the plural of the last or only noun, such as "data warehouses", "foreign keys", "outputs", "take-offs").

---

[90] The word "operating" is an example of an adjective formed from a verb; such adjectives are known as **gerundives** (defined in Section 9.3.2).

[91] Defined in Section 9.6.10.

[92] Defined in Section 9.8.

9.1.3   Gerunds

A **gerund** is a noun such as "working", formed from a **verb** as detailed in Table 18 in Section 9.6.1. All gerunds end in '-ing'.

9.1.4   Plurals

There are various rules for forming plurals. Some nouns do not have plurals, while others do not have a singular form.

9.1.4.1   Mutating plurals

For some words, the plural form is generated by altering the last vowel. These include

- "one foot", "two feet"
- "one mouse", "two mice"
- "one man", "two men"; "one woman", "two women".

The "man"/"men" inflection occurs for all nouns ending in "man" that refer to persons except "German", "human", "Ottoman", "Roman", and "talisman".

9.1.4.2   Foreign plurals

Many of these occur in scientific and technical literature. Only nouns with singular forms of more than one syllable follow the rules in Table 12.

Singular form ending	Plural form	Examples
'us'	replace by 'i' or 'era' or add 'es'	one terminus, two termini one genus, two genera one status, two statuses
'um' or 'on'	replace by 'a'	one maximum, two maxima OR two maximums one memorandum, two memoranda[93] one criterion, two criteria
'a'	add 'e', 'ta', or 's'	one formula, two formulae OR two formulas one schema, two schemata OR two schemas one agenda, two agendas[94]
'ex' or 'ix'	replace by 'ices'	one index, two indices[95] one vertex, two vertices one matrix, two matrices one appendix, two appendices
'is'	replace by 'es'	one axis, two axes one parenthesis, two parentheses
'eau' or 'eu'	add 'x' or 's'	one bureau, two bureaux OR two bureaus one milieu, two milieux OR two milieus

Table 12: Foreign plural forms

9.1.4.3 Irregular plurals

Some words have irregular plurals:

- The plural of "child" is "children".
- The plural of "die" is "dice" (or "dies").
- In UK usage the plural of "penny" is "pence".

---

[93] Despite this, the accepted plural of the abbreviated noun "memo" is "memos".
[94] This is despite "agenda" being derived from a Latin plural noun.
[95] The form "indexes" also occurs.

- The most common plural of "person" is "people", although "persons" may be used in some idioms (like "missing persons" and "displaced persons"), in legal texts, and in some other formal writing.

9.1.4.4 Unmarked plurals

Some words have identical singular and plural forms. Examples are "craft" when referring to a vessel (but not when referring to a skill), "series", "species", "chassis"[96], "ordnance", "offspring", and various words signifying animals, such as "sheep".

9.1.4.5 Regular plurals

These all involve the addition of 's', but in various ways as detailed in Table 13.

---

[96] Although the singular and plural forms of "chassis" are spelled identically, the final 's' is only pronounced in the plural form.

Singular form ending	Plural form	Examples
's', 'ss', 'sh', 'tch', 'x', 'z'	add 'es'	one bus, two buses[97] one process, many processes one wash, a few washes one switch, multiple switches one mix, various mixes one blitz, regular blitzes
'o' or 'i'	add 's' or 'es'[98]	one photo, many photos; one zero, two zeros one alibi, two alibis one embargo, two embargoes OR two embargos
consonant (or 'qu') followed by 'y'	replace 'y' by 'ies'	ability, abilities BUT standby, standbys; layby, laybys
vowel followed by 'y'	add 's'	one day, two days
'e'	add 's'	one site, two sites
'f' or 'fe'	replace 'f' or 'fe' by 'ves' or add 's'	one shelf, two shelves one life, two lives one proof, two proofs
otherwise	add 's'	one column, two columns

Table 13: Regular plural forms

9.1.4.6 Nouns without plurals

Mass nouns[99] do not have plural forms.

The noun "stock" has the plural "stocks" when used to refer to investment in a listed company, but "stock" when used of animals or railway vehicles ("rolling

---

[97] The plural "busses" may be seen occasionally but is generally regarded as incorrect.

[98] Some Italian musical terms ending in 'o' form the plural by replacing the 'o' by 'i', thus "one cello", "two celli" but adding 's' ("cellos") is also acceptable.

[99] Defined in Section 6.2.4.

stock", never *"rolling stocks"). When used of physical assets in a warehouse or retail setting, either plural form may occur.

Most gerunds (such as "programming" or "warehousing") have no plural.

Certain nouns that appear to be plural are in fact singular: "mathematics", "physics", "linguistics", "politics", "news". The noun "statistics" is singular when used of a branch of mathematics, but the noun "statistic" also exists, with the plural "statistics".

9.1.4.7 Nouns without a singular form

Some nouns have only a plural form. These include "staff" (when referring to employees) and "police".

9.1.5 Proper Nouns

A **proper noun** is the name of a single instance of any of the following:

- a person, such as "David Attenborough", "President Kennedy"
- a business or other organization, such as "Microsoft", "the United Nations", "the Senate", "Médecins sans Frontiers", "Harvard University", "Faculty of Science", "Manchester United"
- an ethnic group or nationality, such as "African American", "Hispanic", "Portuguese"
- a place, such as "Asia", "Australia", "the Rockies", "Toronto", "the Atlantic", "the Thames", "Lake Superior", "Mount Everest", "the Sydney Opera House", "the North Pole", "the Equator"
- a natural or artificial language, such as "Japanese", "Esperanto", "Fortran"
- a time period, such as "Monday", "January", "Easter", "the Renaissance"
- a book or other publication, such as "Data Modeling Essentials", "The Washington Post"
- a brand or product, such as "Macintosh", "Prius".

A proper noun may be in plural form but signify a single composite entity instance. For example, it is legitimate to write "the United States is our biggest market" but not *"the United States are our biggest market".

9.2 Determiners

One or more **determiners** may be used before a **common noun** (a noun other than a **proper noun**) to indicate which (or how many) instances of the noun's concept are being referred to. **Adjectives**[100] and **restrictive relative clauses**[101] also do this.

Determiners include:

- **articles**: "a", "an", "the"
- **demonstratives**: "this", "that", "these", "those", used mainly in technical writing to refer to something that has just been discussed, as in "We deferred the remaining enhancements until the next release. This decision was agreed to by management."
- **possessives**: "my", "your", "his", "her", "its", "our", "their", "one's"
- **quantifiers**, such as "all", "both", "some", "many", "few", "several", "no", "more", "most", "the only", and the **cardinal numbers** ("one", "two", and so on), some of which (but not "no" or "the only") can be optionally followed by "of the" (as in "one of the", "some of the")
- **distributives**, such as "any", "each", "either", "every", "neither", "the same", "the other"
- **interrogatives**, such as "which", "what", "whose".

---

[100] Defined in Section 9.3.
[101] Defined in Section 6.1.3.3.

9.3 Adjectives

An **adjective** may either (a) describe an attribute of the person(s) or thing(s) to which a noun refers, or (b) qualify a noun so that it refers only to person(s) or thing(s) with that attribute. For example, "this employee is experienced" describes the employee, whereas "the team consists of experienced employees" states that only experienced employees make up the team.

9.3.1 Compound adjectives

Compound adjectives are formed by combining one or more words to act as an adjective, such as "multi-faceted", "up-to-date".

9.3.2 Gerundives and past participles

Gerundives (or **present participles**) and **past participles** are adjectives derived from verbs. All gerundives end in '-ing', each being identical to the **gerund** formed from the same verb (as described in Table 18 in Section 9.6.1), for example, "closing remarks".

Past participles[102] end in '-ed', '-en', or '-t', for example, "closed case", "written submission", "built environment", "left luggage", "lost cause".

9.3.3 Ordinal numbers

The **ordinal numbers** ("first", "second", "third", and so on) behave as adjectives. Other adjectival words or phrases may be used to define positions in a sequence, including "last", "first or only", "last or only", "second or subsequent", "previous", "next", "every second", "every third".

---

[102] Defined in Section 9.6.1.

9.3.4 Comparative and superlative adjectives

Comparative adjectives indicate a quantitative difference in an attribute, as in "a better solution", "a shorter timeframe". A comparative adjective may also be used in a predicate, as in "This project has taken longer than expected."

Superlative adjectives indicate that the noun qualified refers to the instance that has the attribute more than any other instance in consideration, as in "the best solution", "the shortest distance". A superlative adjective may also be used in a predicate, as in "This project is the longest we have undertaken."

Some adjectives (including ordinals and gerundives) have no comparative or superlative forms.

Comparative and superlative adjectives are formed as detailed in Table 14.

Adjective	Comparative	Superlative	Examples
3 or more syllables, some with 2 syllables	precede by 'more'	precede by 'most'	expensive, more expensive, most expensive
ending in 'e'	add 'r'	add 'st'	large, larger, largest
vowel and single consonant	double consonant, add 'er'	double consonant, add 'est'	big, bigger, biggest
consonant followed by 'y'	replace 'y' by 'ier'	replace 'y' by 'iest'	heavy, heavier, heaviest
otherwise	add 'er'	add 'est'	long, longer, longest

Table 14: Comparative and superlative adjectives

9.4 Pronouns

A **pronoun** is a word (or, occasionally, two words) that may be used instead of a noun phrase.

A **personal pronoun** refers to a noun phrase used elsewhere in a sentence or paragraph rather than repeat the noun phrase. For example, "The project manager stated that she would provide an update that afternoon." rather than "The project manager stated that the project manager would provide an update that afternoon." Personal pronouns may be used in various ways:

- "I", "he", "she", "we", and "they" each refer to an individual person or persons, as the **subject** of a verb, as in "they are responsible", or the **complement** of the verb "be", as in "it is they who are responsible"
- "me", "him", "her", "us", and "them" each refer to an individual person or persons, as the object of a verb or after a preposition, as in "We responded to them by confirming that we would provide them with a report, which would be for them alone."
- "you" refers to the individual person or persons addressed, as subject, complement, object or after a preposition, as in "You have worked effectively, so we are happy to promote you to a position that we believe will be perfect for you."
- "it" (as a personal pronoun) refers to an organization, group of people, or inanimate object, as subject, complement, object or after a preposition, as in "The company stated that it needs to be kept informed. We provided a status report last week and the company is happy with it."

Impersonal pronouns do not substitute for a noun phrase, but instead refer to the context or situation, or a generalized person:

- "it" as in "it has become clear"
- "there" as in "there is" (before a singular noun phrase), "there are" (before a plural noun phrase)
- "one" as in "one can infer"; this may be used to avoid the **passive voice**[103], in this case "it can be inferred".

---

[103] Defined in Section 9.6.4.

Possessive pronouns ("mine", "his", "hers", "its", "ours", "yours", and "theirs") express ownership or possession.

Relative pronouns are used to introduce **relative clauses**[104], which are either:

- **restrictive**, supplying one or more criteria to qualify a noun phrase, as in "we must deliver a system that meets all requirements", or

- **nonrestrictive**, providing more information about a noun phrase, as in "we have installed a new system, which supports more simultaneous users".

As well as "that" and "which", other relative pronouns are "who", "whom", and "whose". The pronouns "which", "who", "whom", and "whose" may also be used as **interrogative pronouns** to introduce a question, as in "Who will be responsible?" "Whom" is used after a preposition, as in "For whom was this a problem?"

In technical writing, **demonstrative pronouns** ("this", "that", "these", "those") refer to something that has just been discussed, as in "We deferred the update until next week. This was to avoid the risk of system unavailability."

Reflexive pronouns ("myself", "yourself", "himself", "herself", "itself", "ourselves", "yourselves", "themselves") refer back to the subject of the clause in which it is used, as in "All team members acquainted themselves with the new operating model."

Reciprocal pronouns ("one another", "each other") are used when an action or relationship is reciprocated, as in "Remote workers communicated with each other daily."

Indefinite pronouns do not refer to any specific person, thing, or amount. These are listed in Table 15.

---

[104] Defined in Section 6.1.3.3.

Persons	Things	Persons or things	Amounts
anybody anyone everybody everyone nobody no one[105] somebody someone	anything everything nothing something	another, each either, enough neither, the other a few, both few, fewer many, several all, any more, most none, some, such others	less little much

Table 15: Indefinite pronouns

A few indefinite pronouns have **possessive forms**:

- all indefinite pronouns referring to persons, as in "this is everyone's responsibility", "nobody's job is affected", and "others' views may differ"
- "another" and "the other", as in "another's argument was that …" and "the other's position was more understandable".

9.5 Prepositions

A **preposition** is one or more words that may be used between two nouns (with a possible intervening verb) to express either:

- a relationship between the objects referenced by the two nouns, as with "on" in "he is on the selection committee", or
- movement by the object referenced by the first noun with respect to the object referenced by the second noun, as with "into" in "the row is inserted into the table".

---

[105] "No-one" is acceptable in all but a few communities. "Noone" is universally regarded as incorrect.

A preposition may also be used:

- directly after a noun, as in "the fields on this form"
- before a **pronoun**[106], as in "This is the method preferred by us."

Most relationships expressed using a preposition belong to one of the following categories:

1. **locational**, such as "on", "in", "above", "below", "in front of", "behind", "beside", "within", "between", "to" (as in "to Head Office"), "into", "onto"
2. **temporal**, such as "before", "after", "during"
3. **causative**, such as "due to", "because of", "as a result of"
4. **beneficiary**, such as "for", "to" (as in "to the recipient")
5. **possessive**, such as "of", "belonging to"
6. **perspective**, such as "as", "in the form of"
7. **comparative**, such as "the same as", "different from"[107], "similar to", "more than", "less than", "fewer than", "equal to", "later than", "earlier than", "the same time as", "between", "from", "to" (as in "from 1 to 10"), "up to", "unequal to".

Prepositions may be combined using logical operators (as in "in and around", "on or above") or negated (as in "not equal to").

---

[106] Defined in Section 9.4.

[107] An alternative form is "different to". The use of "different than" as a preposition is regarded as incorrect in UK English, although a clause such as "having a different perspective than you" (in which "different" is used as an adjective) is acceptable.

Prepositions are often used in **idioms**, such as "in progress", "out of date", "below the acceptable minimum", where their meaning may differ from their literal meaning.

Some prepositions may also act as **conjunctions**[108]. For example, "after" acts as a preposition in "after retrieval of the data" and "after retrieving the data" but as a conjunction in "after the data was retrieved".

9.6 Verbs

Verbs refer to various types of occurrences, namely:

- actions, such as "build", as in "build a system"
- events, such as "fail", as in "the system may fail"
- mental activities and behaviors, such as "know", "understand", "respect", or "disagree"
- verbal activities, such as "inform", "explain", "specify", or "ask"
- situations, such as those expressed using "be" or "have".

Every verb other than a **modal** ("can", "could", "may", "might", "must", "shall", "should", "will", "would") exhibits two behaviors, which only verbs exhibit:

1. The form after "he", "she", "it", or a singular noun (for example, "is" and "specifies") is different to the form after "they" or a plural noun ("are" and "specify" in these two examples).

2. It has a form (the **infinitive**) that may follow any modal. Except for "is"/"are" (for which the infinitive form is "be"), the infinitive form of all verbs is the same as the form after "they" or a plural noun, as in "he must be here" or "he can specify how this should be done".

---

[108] Defined in Section 9.7.

9.6.1 Verb forms

All verbs except "be", "beware", and the modals have the following forms:

1. the **base form**[109] (the form listed in a dictionary), which is used
    - as the **infinitive** immediately after "to" or a modal, as in "we intend to begin soon", "this may begin whenever required"
    - immediately after "I", "we", "you", "they", "these", "those", or a plural noun, when expressing a current occurrence or condition (the **default present form**), as in "we begin soon"
2. the **third person present form** used immediately after "he", "she", "it", "this", "that", or a singular noun, when expressing a current occurrence or situation, as in "the environment begins to deteriorate", formed as detailed in Table 16
3. the **simple past form** used immediately after any noun or pronoun (singular or plural), when expressing a past occurrence or situation, as in "the system began to exhibit anomalies", formed as detailed in Table 17
4. the **past participle** form used immediately after "have", "has", or "had", as in "we had begun to observe discrepancies"; this is identical to the simple past form except for some **irregular verbs**[110]
5. the **present participle** form, ending in "ing", as in "we are beginning to see an increase in such cases", formed as detailed in Table 18.

Each modal (and the verb "beware") has only one form.

---

[109] This is also known as the **bare form** or **plain form**.
[110] See Section 9.6.2.

Infinitive form ending	Form after "he", "she", "it", or a singular noun	Examples
's', 'ss', 'sh', 'tch'	add 'es'	we process, she processes we wish, he wishes we switch, she switches
'o'	add 'es'	they embargo, the government embargoes
consonant followed by 'y'	replace 'y' by 'ies'	we modify, he modifies
otherwise (except for "be", "beware")	add 's'	they create, the process creates

Table 16: third person present form

Infinitive form ending	Simple past form	Examples
'e'	add 'd'	create, created
consonant followed by 'y'	replace 'y' by 'ied'	modify, modified
long vowel followed by 'r'	add 'red'	recur, recurred; infer, inferred
'el'	(US English) add 'ed' (UK English) add 'led'	model, modeled; cancel, canceled model, modelled; cancel, cancelled
short vowel followed by 's'	add 'ing'	focus, focused[111]
short vowel followed by other consonant	double the consonant and add 'ed'	drop, dropped
'c'	add 'ked'	bivouac, bivouacked
otherwise	add 'ed'	adapt, adapted; roll, rolled

Table 17: Simple past form

---

[111] The form "focussed" is acceptable in some organizations.

Infinitive form ending	Present participle	Examples
'ie'	replace 'ie' by 'ying'	vie, vying
'e' not preceded by 'i'	replace 'e' by 'ing'	create, creating
long vowel followed by 'r'	add 'ring'	recur, recurring; infer, inferring
'el'	(US English) add 'ing' (UK English) add 'ling'	model, modeling; cancel, canceling model, modelling; cancel, cancelling
short vowel followed by 's'	add 'ing'	focus, focusing[112]
short vowel followed by other consonant	double the consonant and add 'ing'	running
otherwise	add 'ing'	adapt, adapting; roll, rolling

Table 18: Present participle

9.6.2 Irregular verbs

The verb "be" has the following forms:

1. the **base form** "be", used as the **infinitive** (immediately after "to" or a modal), as in "it needs to be updated today", "this may be so"

2. "**am**", the form used immediately after "I", when expressing a current fact, as in "I am pleased to report that …"

3. "**is**", the form used immediately after "he", "she", "it", or a singular noun or demonstrative pronoun, when expressing a current fact, as in "the system is live", "this is the only version"

4. "**are**", the form used immediately after "we", "you", "they", or a plural noun or demonstrative pronoun, when expressing a current fact, as in "they are the best people for the job"

5. "**was**", the form used immediately after "he", "she", "it", or a singular noun or demonstrative pronoun, when expressing a past fact, as in "the system was obsolete"

---

[112] The form "focussing" is acceptable in some organizations.

6. "were", the form used immediately after "we", "you", "they", or a plural noun or demonstrative pronoun, when expressing a past fact, as in "they were obsolete"
7. "been", the **past participle** form used immediately after "have", "has", or "had", as in "she has been assigned to this project from the beginning"
8. "being", the **present participle** form, as in "that being so".

There are other verbs with (a) a **simple past form** with a different final vowel from that of the **base form**, and (b) different simple past and **past participle** forms (as defined in Section 9.6.1). Table 19 lists the most common of these in technical or business writing.

Infinitive	Simple past	Past participle	Infinitive	Simple past	Past participle
arise	arose	arisen	give	gave	given
become	became	become	go	went	gone
begin	began	begun	grow	grew	grown
choose	chose	chosen	hide	hid	hidden
come	came	come	know	knew	known
do	did	done	ring	rang	rung
draw	drew	drawn	run	ran	run
drive	drove	driven	see	saw	seen
fall	fell	fallen	show	showed	shown
fly	flew	flown	speak	spoke	spoken
forget	forgot	forgotten	take	took	taken
freeze	froze	frozen	wear	wore	worn
get	got	got or gotten	write	wrote	written

Table 19: Irregular verbs with different simple past and past participle forms

There are also verbs with (a) a **simple past form** with a different final vowel and/or consonant(s) from those of the **base form**, but (b) the same simple past and **past participle** forms. Table 20 lists the most common of these in technical or business writing.

Infinitive	Past forms
bring	brought
build	built
buy	bought
catch	caught
feel	felt
find	found
have	had
hear	heard
hold	held
keep	kept

Infinitive	Past forms
lay	laid
lead	led
leave	left
lose	lost
make	made
mean	meant
meet	met
pay	paid
say	said
seek	sought

Infinitive	Past forms
sell	sold
send	sent
sit	sat
spend	spent
stand	stood
teach	taught
tell	told
think	thought
understand	understood
win	won

Table 20: Irregular verbs with the same simple past and past participle forms

There are also verbs with identical base, simple past and past participle forms. The most common of these in technical or business writing are "bid", "broadcast", "cast", "cost", "cut", "forecast"[113], "let", "put", "read", "set", and "shut".

Some verbs have alternative spellings of the simple past and past participle. These include "earn" with "earned" or "earnt", "learn" with "learned" or "learnt", and "spell" with "spelled" or "spelt". In general, US usage prefers the '-ed' ending while UK usage prefers the '-t' ending. However, some style guides favor the '-ed' ending for the simple past and the '-t' ending for the past participle. A third convention favors the '-ed' ending when the duration of the action is important, and the '-t' ending when it is not.

---

[113] Some style guides and dictionaries accept "forecasted" as an alternative.

9.6.3 Tenses

Tenses enable us to express whether something occurs or exists now or in the past or future, whether it is continuous, and whether it is complete.

9.6.3.1 Simple present

The **simple present** is used if something occurs or exists at the time of writing. Note that, if it might have ceased or changed by the time a document is read, a statement using the simple present tense should be qualified by "at the time of writing", as in "annual inflation is at 3% at the time of writing".

For verbs other than "be", the simple present tense uses the base form of the verb (as in "I begin"), except after "he", "she", "it", or a **singular noun** or **demonstrative pronoun**, when a form ending in '-s' is used.[114]

For the verb "be", the simple present tense uses "am" after "I", "are" after "you", "is" after "he", "she", "it", or a **singular noun** or **demonstrative pronoun**, and "are" after a **plural noun** or pronoun.

9.6.3.2 Simple future

The **simple future** is used when something is expected to occur later than the time of writing; it does not imply that it has not already occurred. It uses "will" followed by the **base form**, as in "It will be the largest operations center in the state."

---

[114] See Table 16 in Section 9.6.1. The base form must be used after "they" even if "they" is being used as a gender-neutral singular pronoun, thus "Each student must advise the university if they have decided to withdraw."

The simple present may also be used for occurrences that are expected to come into effect in future. For example, "the project team finishes next week" may be an acceptable alternative to "the project team will finish next week".

9.6.3.3 Simple past

The **simple past** is used if an event or action both started and finished in the past, such as "Version 2.3 was released in May". For an event or action that started in the past and continues in the present, the **present perfect** (see next section) should be used.

9.6.3.4 Perfect tenses

There are various **perfect** tenses:

- The **present perfect** is used for something that started in the past and is still in effect, as in "the problem has arisen", "we have become aware of the problem this week", "we have been aware of this problem".

- The **past perfect** is used for something that took place before some other past occurrence, stated or unstated, as in "this problem had arisen previously", "this problem had arisen before we finished development".

- The **future perfect** is used for something that is expected to take place before some other future occurrence, stated or unstated, as in "this problem will have arisen by the conclusion of testing".

Each uses the **past participle**, in this case "arisen". For **regular verbs** the past participle is the same as the simple past, thus "we employ", "we employed", "we have employed". This is also true of some (but not all) irregular verbs, as detailed in Section 9.6.2.

9.6.3.5 Progressive tenses

There are various **progressive tenses** (also known as **continuous tenses**), used for ongoing occurrences:

- the **present continuous** (as in "this problem is causing concern"), used for something happening at the time of writing
- the **future continuous** (as in "we will be enhancing the system over the next 6 months"), used for something expected to happen after the time of writing
- the **simple past continuous** (as in "this problem was causing concern"), used for something that happened before the time of writing but is no longer happening
- the **present perfect continuous** (as in "this problem has been causing concern"), used for something that happened before the time of writing and is still happening
- the **past perfect continuous** (as in "this problem had been causing concern"), used for something that took place before some other past occurrence, stated or unstated
- the **future perfect continuous** (as in "it will have been operating for 12 months"), used for something that is expected to take place before some other future occurrence, stated or unstated.[115]

Each uses the **present participle** ("causing", "enhancing", or "operating" in these examples), formed as detailed in Table 18 in Section 9.6.1.

Stative verbs cannot be used in any of the progressive tenses. Stative verbs describe ongoing situations (such as "own", "exist"), mental states (such as

---

[115] Some uses of future continuous forms (e.g., *"this problem will be causing concern", *"this problem will have been causing concern") are nonstandard.

"know", "understand", "believe"), emotions (such as "prefer"), and senses (such as like "see", "hear"). "We understand that this may exceed the budget" is correct, but not *"We are understanding that this may exceed the budget."

A few verbs have both stative and non-stative meanings. "We see this regularly" is stative, representing an ongoing situation. "We are seeing an increase in these errors" is progressive, representing a changing situation.

9.6.3.6   Other tense-like verb constructions

There are other verb constructions:

- "be about to" may be used to refer to something that is or was imminent, as in "We are about to migrate all data to the new platform."
- "be to" may be used (in the form "were to") in the **subjunctive mood**[116], as in "If it were to fail, data might be corrupted."
- "go to" may be used to refer to an intended action, as in "we are going to improve on this performance."
- "used to" may be used to refer to something which no longer occurs or exists, as in "The company used to post results quarterly."

9.6.4   Active and passive voice

All examples so far in this chapter have been in the **active voice**. In each example involving a verb expressing an action, the subject of the sentence refers to the **actor** (the person or thing that performed the action). Thus, in "the application regularly backs up the database", "application" is the subject of the sentence and performs the action, whereas "database" is the direct object of the sentence and is the recipient of the action.

---

[116] Defined in Section 9.6.6.3.

In the **passive voice**, the recipient of the action is made the subject of the sentence, as in "the database is backed up regularly by the application." Verbs in the passive voice use a form of the verb "be" followed by the **past participle**[117], in this case "is backed up". Most tenses may be used in the passive, thus "it is used", "it will be used", "it was used", "it has been used", "it had been used", "it will have been used", "it is being used", "it was being used" (but not other progressive forms).

Where an actor is identified, the noun specifying the actor appears after the passive verb and the preposition "by", as in "Customers have been overcharged by many financial institutions."

9.6.5 Negation

All examples so far in this chapter are assertions that something is, was, or will be the case. The addition of "not" changes a phrase to one that asserts that something is not, was not, or will not be the case. Depending on the verb, it may only be negated in the simple present or past tense in one of two ways:

- The verb "be" and the **modals**[118] may be followed by "not", as in "it is not clear ..." or "this must not be allowed to occur". The verbs "have" and "do" may only be followed by "not" when acting as auxiliaries, as in "this has not occurred" or "this does not meet requirements". If "have" or "do" is acting as a main verb rather than an auxiliary, it must be preceded by "do not", "does not", or "did not" (as appropriate). Thus "this department does not have sufficient resources" rather than *"this department has not sufficient resources"[119]; "he does not do the necessary work" rather than *"he does not the necessary work".

---

[117] Defined in Section 9.6.1.

[118] Defined in Section 9.6.8.

[119] An alternative without "not" is "this department has insufficient resources".

- Any other verb may only be preceded by "do not", "does not", or "did not", as in "this does not represent the complete picture".

In other tenses, the assertion is negated by following the first or only auxiliary by "not". For example, "this will not work", "this has not worked", "this had not worked", "this will not have worked", "this is not causing concern", "we will not be enhancing the system", "this was not causing concern", "this has not been causing concern", "this had not been causing concern", "it will not have been operating for sufficient time".

9.6.6 Mood

All examples so far in this chapter are assertions that something is, was or will be the case, or is not, was not or will not be the case. Such sentences are in the **indicative mood**. There are three other moods: **interrogative**, **imperative**, and **subjunctive**.

9.6.6.1 Interrogative mood

Sentences in the **interrogative mood** are questions. Indicative mood sentences that use (a) the simple present or past tense, and (b) the verb "be" or a **modal**[120] are made interrogative by reversing the order of the verb and subject. Thus:

- "This is the right approach." becomes "Is this the right approach?"
- "The chosen approach was effective." becomes "Was the chosen approach effective?"
- "The project must continue." becomes "Must the project continue?"

---

[120] Defined in Section 9.6.8.

Sentences in the **simple present** or **past** tense with a verb other than **"be"** or a modal are made interrogative by (a) starting with **"do", "does"** or **"did"**, and (b) changing the verb to the **infinitive** form. Thus:

- "The specification details all data formats." becomes "Does the specification detail all data formats?"
- "The application failed." becomes "Did the application fail?"

Sentences in other tenses are made interrogative by reversing the order of the first auxiliary verb and subject. Thus:

- "That will work." becomes "Will that work?"
- "That has worked." becomes "Has that worked?"
- "That had worked." becomes "Had that worked?"
- "That will have worked." becomes "Will that have worked?"

9.6.6.2   Imperative mood

The **imperative mood** is used for instructions, such as "Click on the 'Save' button." It uses the **base form** (the form listed in a dictionary).

The imperative mood is inappropriate in most technical or business writing. However:

- it is common in user manuals and Standard Operating Procedures
- in technical writing generally, it is permissible to use **"refer to"** as an instruction to readers to refer to another document or another section in the same document.
- it may also be used in office communications such as emails, where it is common to precede each instruction by **"please"**, as in "Please reply by close of business tomorrow."

9.6.6.3 Subjunctive mood

The **subjunctive mood** is used for:

- clauses starting with "if" expressing a condition that is contrary to fact, as in "If this were the case, we would have taken appropriate action."
- wishes, commands, proposals, requests, suggestions, or statements of necessity, as in "We requested that he implement the recommendation." and "It is necessary that the database be backed up regularly."

In these examples, "were", "attend", and "be" are used rather than "was", "attends" and "is". This is because, for verbs other than "be", the only form used in the subjunctive mood is the base form (the form listed in a dictionary), while, for the verb "be", the only forms used in the subjunctive mood are "be" and "were".

There are also various stock phrases which use the subjunctive mood, including "as it were", "be that as it may", "if need be", "suffice it to say".

A clause that starts with "if" and uses the subjunctive "were" may be rephrased by moving "were" to the start in place of "if". For example, "if it were to fail." may be rephrased "were it to fail". Note that "were" in these clauses does not refer to the past but to a potential future.

9.6.7 Primary auxiliaries

We have already seen that "be" may be used to form progressive tenses and the passive voice, "have" to form perfect tenses, and "do" used for negation or the interrogative mood.

Each of these may also be used as a main verb, as in "She is the project manager.", "He has the authority.", and "They do it well."

9.6.8 Modals

The **modals** in English are "can", "could", "may", "might", "must", "shall", "should", "will", "would". They have two characteristics:

- Each has only one form, rather than the separate forms listed in Section 9.6.1.
- They cannot be used alone but must be used with a main verb. The main verb may be implied in a sentence following a direct or indirect question, as in "Will this work? Yes, it will." or "There may be concern that this will not work. We are confident that it will."

9.6.8.1 Can, could

The verb "can" is used to express ability or capacity, as in "This system can monitor delays."[121]

The verb "could" may be used to express:

- an ability or capacity which existed in the past, as in "We could estimate the likely impact."
- what is possible or may happen, as in "This could cost more than the total budget."

Inability or impossibility is signified by "cannot" or "could not", as in "The data cannot be retrieved. We could not foresee this."

To express an ability or capacity using a tense other than simple present or past, use the compound verb "be able to", as in "We have been able to establish the cause of the outage."

---

[121] This verb is not to be confused with the main verb "can", as in "The company cans fruit."

9.6.8.2 May, might

The verb "may" is used to express

- a possibility, as in "We may select this option." (meaning "It is possible that we will select this option.")
- a permission, as in "We may select this option" (meaning "We are allowed to select this option.")

A possibility may also be expressed using "might" instead of "may". If the possibility is quite likely, you may use "may well" or "might well", as in "This may well be the best approach."

If it is possible that something is not true, you may use "might not", as in "This might not work."

To express the possibility that something happened (or was the case) in the past, use "may have" or "might have", as in "This might have skewed the results."

To express the possibility that something did not happen (or was not the case), use "may not have" or "might not have", as in "This data may not have been completely captured."

9.6.8.3 Must

The verb "must" is used to express:

- an obligation, as in "This data must be deleted."
- a logical conclusion or belief, as in "This data must have been deleted."

To express an obligation using a tense other than simple present, use the compound verb "be obliged to" or (less formally) "have to", as in "At that time Customers did not have to supply an Individual Taxpayer Identification Number."

Note that "must not" expresses a prohibition, as in "Passengers must not use mobile phones while passing through Border Control."

If there is no obligation, use "be not obliged to" or (less formally) "do not have to", as in "Customers are not obliged to enter this data." or "It does not have to be completed today."

9.6.8.4 Shall, should

The verbs "shall" and "will" were once governed by complex rules for expressing various meanings. However, nowadays "shall" is most commonly used to express contractual obligations, as in "Each of the parties hereto shall give the other prompt written notice of any claims." By contrast, "will" expresses simple assertions about the future.

The verb "should" is used to express:

- hypothetical situations, as in "if the transaction should fail" or "should the transaction fail"
- desirable actions, features or situations, as in "all team members should attend this meeting".

9.6.8.5 Will, would

The verb "will" is used to express simple assertions about the future, as in "We will complete the project on time."

The verb "would" is used to express:

- past beliefs about the future, as in "At the start of the project, we believed it would be necessary to assemble a larger team."
- hypotheses, as in "That would be more expensive to implement."
- conditional situations, as in "We would finish the data conversion sooner if we could control our own permissions."

9.6.9 Semi-modal verbs

These are verbs that sometimes behave as modals but not always.

9.6.9.1 Dare

"Dare" may be used as a main verb, as in "She dares to disagree." It may also be used as a modal, as in "He dare not disagree."

9.6.9.2 Need

"Need" is mostly used as a main verb, as in "The company needs to expand its product line." It may also be used as a modal, as in "It need not change."

9.6.9.3 Ought to

"Ought to" (like the modals) has only one form and cannot be used alone (except when a main verb is implied in a sentence following a direct or indirect question, as in "Should we finish now? We ought to."). It may be used to indicate

- advice, as in "The database ought to be backed up more often."
- expectation, as in "The testing ought to be complete by the end of the week."

If something is not expected or advisable, "ought not to" may be used, as in "We ought not to ignore this possibility."

"Should" may replace "ought to" in either usage; "should not" may similarly replace "ought not to".

9.6.9.4 Used to

"Used to" may be used as a main verb (meaning "accustomed to"), as in "We are used to seeing this problem." or "We have become used to having to deal with this." It may also be used as a modal, to indicate an occurrence or condition that is no longer the case, as in "This used to be the only way to input data."

9.6.10 Phrasal verbs

A **phrasal verb** is a verb followed by one or more adverbs or prepositions which modify the meaning of the verb, such as **"back up"** and **"work through"**. A verb may be followed by an adverb and a preposition, as in **"go along with"** or **"run out of"**.

The meanings of most phrasal verbs are idiomatic, in that they do not derive from the meanings of the verb and the adverb or preposition. For example, there is no sense of elevation in most phrasal verbs including **"up"**. Some phrasal verbs have both literal and idiomatic meanings. For example, **"look up"** means "look upwards" (literal) or "search for" (idiomatic).

9.6.11 Verbs before "that", "if", "whether", or "to"

Verbs that assert the truth of a proposition are usually followed by "that". These include **"assert"**, **"believe"**, **"hypothesize"**, **"imply"**, **"report"**, and **"state"**, as in "the stakeholder stated that this was required". Note that "that" may often be omitted from after such verbs, as in **"The stakeholder stated this was required."**

Verbs that question the truth of a proposition are followed by "if", "whether" or "that". These include **"ask"**, **"question"**, and **"check"**, as in **"I asked if this were true"**, **"she questioned whether this was required"**, or **"the reviewer checked that all requirements were included."**

Inferences may be introduced by "it follows that", as in **"It follows that a hash key cannot be used."**

The verb "expect" may be used in four ways: (a) followed by a noun, as in **"expect a resolution"**, (b) followed by "that", as in **"expect that it be resolved"**, (c) followed by a clause, as in **"expect all matters to be resolved"**, or (d) followed by "to", as in **"expect to resolve all matters"**.

Like "expect", many verbs may be used before "to" and the **infinitive** of another verb. These include "afford", "agree", "aim", "appear", "arrange", "attempt", "consent", "decide", "endeavor", "fail", "guarantee", "intend", "manage", "need", "plan", "prepare", "proceed", "try", and "undertake".

9.6.12 Verbs before clauses

Some verbs may be followed by clauses rather than objects, as in "This appears to be the norm."

9.7 Conjunctions

9.7.1 Coordinating conjunctions

The **coordinating conjunctions** "and", "but", "nor", "or", "so", and "yet"[122] join **independent clauses**[123], as in "Testing is complete, and the new version will be released tomorrow." In addition, "and" and "or" may join phrases, as described in Section 9.9.8.

9.7.2 Subordinating conjunctions

A **subordinating conjunction** introduces a **dependent clause**[124] before or after an independent clause, as in "As this method works, we will use it." or "We will use this method as it works." These conjunctions serve various purposes:

- reason: "as", "because", "in order that", "since", "so that"

---

[122] Many sources also list "for" as a coordinating conjunction with the same meaning as "because", but it is no longer in common use.
[123] Defined in Section 6.1.3.
[124] Defined in Section 6.1.3.

- comparison: "although", "as much as", "even though", "just as", "though", "whereas"
- condition: "even if", "except that", "if", "in case", "only if", "provided", "provided that", "unless"
- place: "where", "wherever"
- time: "after", "as", "as soon as", "as long as", "before", "by the time", "every time", "in the event that", "now that", "once", "since", "until", "when", "whenever", "while"
- miscellaneous: "as though", "except that", "how", "than", "that", "whether", "whether or not", "what", "which", "who", "why".

9.8 Adverbs

Adverbs modify words of various classes, by providing additional information (such as the manner, time, frequency, place, certainty, or extent) about the action or relationship represented by the verb or clause:

- **verbs**, as with "today" in "the new version was released today"
- **adjectives**, as with "too" in "this approach is too risky"
- other adverbs, as with "more" in "more recently"
- **determiners**, as with "possibly" in "this is possibly the only feasible option"
- **prepositional phrases**, as with "almost" in "this was almost over budget"
- entire **clauses**, as with "however" in "however this is managed, it must be done this week".

Many adverbs are formed from adjectives, as illustrated in Table 21. There are exceptions: the adverb equivalent to "good" is "well".

Adjective ending	Adverb	Examples
'y'	replace 'y' by 'ily'	easy, easily
'le'	replace 'le' by 'ly'	possible, possibly
'ic' (except public)	add 'ally'	historic, historically public, publicly
otherwise (except good)	add 'ly'	careful, carefully wrong, wrongly

Table 21: Formation of adverbs from adjectives

Like adjectives, most adverbs have comparative and superlative forms[125]. Where they exist, these are formed by writing "more" or "most" before the adverb, as in "more easily" and "most productively".

9.9 Phrases

Sentences consist of **clauses**, which in turn consist of **phrases**, which in turn consist of **words**, other phrases, and even clauses. The following subsections list options for constructing each type of phrase. Except for **finite verb phrases**, these options are set out in tables in which:

- the **head word** (the mandatory component of each phrase) is in a central column, marked in bold
- words, phrases, and clauses that may optionally precede the head word are in a column or columns to the left of the central column
- words, phrases, and clauses that may optionally follow the head word are in a column or columns to the right of the central column
- examples of that type of phrase are included in the same table or a separate table.

---

[125] See Section 9.3.4.

9.9.1 Noun phrases

Preceding words	Head word	Following words
determiner and/or adjective phrase	noun	prepositional phrase, relative clause, or nonfinite verb phrase
	pronoun	prepositional phrase, participial phrase, or relative clause

Table 22: Noun phrase formation

Example	Pattern
databases	noun
these databases	determiner + noun
these relational databases	determiner + adjective phrase + noun
the databases installed on this server	determiner + noun + participial phrase
the databases being replaced	determiner + noun + participial phrase
the databases under review	determiner + noun + prepositional phrase
the databases that were replaced	determiner + noun + relative clause
the last row to be deleted	determiner + adjective phrase + noun + infinitive phrase
permission to drop the table	noun + infinitive phrase
they	pronoun
those involved	pronoun + participial phrase
those in contention	pronoun + prepositional phrase
those that were deleted	pronoun + relative clause
what we now know	pronoun + relative clause (equivalent to that which we now know)

Table 23: Noun phrase examples

9.9.2 Finite verb phrases

Each sentence must include at least one **independent clause**, which must include a **finite verb phrase**[126], which may be any of the following:

- a **present form**, such as "writes", "write"[127]
- the **simple past form**, such as "wrote"
- a combination of:
    - a form of "have", "be", "do", and/or a **modal** ("can", "could", "may", "might", "must", "shall", "should", "will", or "would") and
    - the **past participle**, **present participle**, or **base form**[128]

  that fits one of the following templates:
    - "have"/"has"/"had"/"will have" + past participle, as in "has written"
    - "is"/"are"/"am"/"was"/"will be"/"has been"/ "have been", "had been", "will have been" + present participle, as in "are writing"
    - "is"/"are"/"am"/"was"/"will be"/"has been"/ "have been", "had been", "will have been" + past participle, as in "has been written"
    - "do"/"does"/"did" + base form, as in "did write"
    - modal + base form, as in "must write"
    - modal + "have" + past participle, as in "may have written"
    - modal + "be" + present participle, as in "should be writing"
    - modal + "be" + past participle, as in "would be written"
    - modal + "have been" + present participle, as in "could have been writing"
    - modal + "have been" + past participle, as in "might have been written"

---

[126] This book uses the traditional meaning of **verb phrase** rather than the meaning used in generative grammar, for which traditional grammar uses the term **predicate**.

[127] While some sources assert that the present and simple past forms are not verb phrases but simply verbs, it seems reasonable to allow a verb phrase to consist of just a verb, given that those same sources assert that a noun phrase can consist of just a noun.

[128] Defined in Section 9.6.1.

- any of the above followed (if the verb allows) by an **infinitive phrase**, as in "intends to show", "had intended to show"
- the following negative constructions:
    - "does not" + base form, such as "does not see"
    - "did not" + base form, such as "did not see"
    - one of the above templates, with "not" after "have", "be", "do", or the modal, whichever appears first, such as "has not seen", "is not seeing", "is not seen", "does not see", "could not see", "could not have seen", "could not have been seen".

9.9.3 Nonfinite verb phrases

There are other, **nonfinite**, verb phrases which may be used in sentences: **present participial phrases**, **past participial phrases**, and **infinitive phrases**.

9.9.3.1 Present participial phrases

Preceding words	Head word	Following words	Examples
not	present participle	noun phrase	summarizing the options
	being	past participle + prepositional phrase	not being considered for inclusion
	having	past participle + noun phrase	having completed all updates
	having been	past participle + prepositional phrase	having been compromised by the outage

Table 24: Present participial phrase formation and examples

9.9.3.2 Past participial phrases

Preceding words	Head word	Following words	Examples
not and/or adverb phrase	past participle		always included not followed up
		adjective phrase	thought impossible not considered relevant
		prepositional phrase	newly added to the data not included in this test

Table 25: Past participial phrase formation and examples

9.9.3.3 Infinitive phrases

Head word	Examples
to + **verb base form**	to finish
to be + **past participle**	to be deleted

Table 26: Infinitive phrase formation and examples

9.9.4 Adjective phrases

Adjectives may be used in either of two ways:

- A **predicative adjective** describes an attribute of the person(s) or thing(s) to which a noun refers, as in "this employee is experienced"

- An **attributive adjective** qualifies a noun so that it refers only to person(s) or thing(s) with that attribute, as in "the team consists of experienced employees", meaning only experienced employees make up the team.

Preceding words	Head word	Following words	Examples
not and/or adverb phrase	**adjective**	adverb phrase	fast faster fastest not very fast fast enough
	comparative adjective	than + adjective	more than sufficient

Table 27: Attributive adjective phrase formation and examples

Preceding words	Head word	Following words	Examples
not and/or adverb phrase	**adjective**	adverb phrase	successful more successful most successful
		prepositional phrase	effective in practice
		infinitive phrase	ready to install
	comparative adjective	than + adjective phrase	more than necessary faster than previously experienced
		than + adverb phrase	faster than previously
		than + noun phrase and/or participial phrase	better than the alternative easier than creating a new table

Table 28: Predicative adjective phrase formation and examples

9.9.5 Adverb phrases

Preceding words	Head word	Following words	Examples
not and/or adverbs	**adverb**	prepositional phrase	soon not completely very soon unfortunately for the team

Table 29: Adverb phrase formation and examples

9.9.6 Prepositional phrases

Preceding words	Head word	Following words[129]	Examples
adverb phrase	**preposition**	noun phrase	in this table
		present participial phrase	immediately after loading the data

Table 30: Prepositional phrase formation and examples

9.9.7 Absolute phrases

Head word	Following words	Examples
noun phrase	adjective phrase	the rebuild complete
	present participial phrase	the meeting resuming
	past participial phrase	the project cancelled

Table 31: Absolute phrase formation and examples

9.9.8 Combining phrases using logical conjunctions

Phrases of a given type may be combined in a clause using logical conjunctions:

- Any two phrases of the same type may be joined by "and" or "or", as in "tables and columns", "commits or rolls back", "would have been dropped and recreated", "fast and accurate", "effectively and efficiently", "on or around".

- In most cases (one exception being **attributive adjective phrases**), two phrases of the same type may be joined by:
  - "yet", as in "on time yet over budget"
  - "both" before the first and "and" before the second, as in "was both designed and built"
  - "either" before the first and "or" before the second, as in "has either passed or failed"

---

[129] A following noun phrase or present participial phrase is mandatory in a prepositional phrase.

- o "neither" before the first and "nor" before the second, as in "had neither sent nor received"
  - o "not" before the first and "but" before the second, as in "have not terminated but extended"
  - o "not only" before the first and "but" or "but also" before the second, as in "not only on time but within budget"
  - o "whether" before the first and "or" before the second, as in "whether it has passed or failed".
- In most cases (again except for attributive adjective phrases), three or more phrases may be joined, with commas between consecutive phrases and ", and" or ", or" before the last phrase, as in "will have extracted, transformed, and loaded" or "effectively, efficiently, and on time".[130]

9.9.8.1 Combining verb phrases

When combining two verb phrases (which must be of the same **tense**)[131]:

- if using just "and" or "or", all but the last verb is omitted from the second verb phrase: thus "would have been dropped and recreated" rather than "would have been dropped and would have been recreated"
- "both", "either" , "neither" , or "not", is inserted after the initial verb in the first verb phrase, and only the participle of the second verb phrase is written; thus "was both designed and built" rather than *"both was designed and was built".

---

[130] However, see Section 6.3.4 for an example where the inclusion of a comma before "and" or "or" may introduce ambiguity.

[131] See Section 9.6.3.

9.9.8.2 Combining attributive adjective phrases

Attributive adjective phrases may be combined using logical conjunctions as follows[132]:

- two adjective phrases joined by "and" or "or", such as "current or future"
- three or more adjective phrases with commas between consecutive adjective phrases and ", and" or ", or" before the last adjective phrase, such as "past, present, or future".[133]

---

[132] This is in addition to the use of multiple adjective phrases as discussed in Section 6.2.2.2.

[133] However, see Section 6.3.4 for an example where the inclusion of a comma before "and" or "or" may introduce ambiguity.

Suggested Reading

Most English-speaking countries have produced their own style guides:

- Australia:
    - Australian Government Style Manual
    - Australian Style Guide
- Canada:
    - The Canadian Press Stylebook
    - The Canadian style: a guide to writing and editing
- South Africa:
    - The South African Style Guide
- UK:
    - New Oxford Style Manual (3rd ed.)
    - Copy-editing: The Cambridge Handbook for Editors, Authors and Publishers
- US:
    - The Associated Press Stylebook
    - The Chicago Manual of Style

International bodies have also created style guides for publications in English:

- International Organization for Standardization Style Guide
- English Style Guide: A handbook for authors and translators in the European Commission

The following books provide detailed advice about English language usage:

- Australia:
    - Watson, D. (2003). *Death Sentence*. Knopf.
    - Watson, D. (2004). *Weasel Words*. Knopf.

- UK:
    - Fowler, H. W. (1996). *Modern English Usage* (3rd ed.). Oxford University Press.
    - Gowers, E. (1987). *The Complete Plain Words* (3rd ed.). Penguin Books.
- US:
    - Plain Writing Act of 2010
    - Strunk, W., & White, E. B. (1999). *The Elements of Style* (4th ed.). Longman
- International:
    - Partridge, E. (1973). *Usage and Abusage*. Penguin Books

Index

Numbers in bold indicate pages in which the term is defined or explained; numbers in italics indicate references in footnotes.

abbreviation, 24, 26, **72–74**, 80, 81, 141, 145
ability, 218
absolute phrase, **113**, 115, 231
acronym, *72*
active voice, 136, **213**
activity diagram, 99
actor, 136, 213, 214
adjective, **50**, 63, 111, 112, 114, **121**, 134, 135, 150, 151, 154, 169, 171, 173, 174, 177, 184, 185, 188, 191, 197, **198–99**, 198, *203*, 224, 225, 229, 230, 231
    attributive, **121**, 122, **229**
    comparative, 113, 121, 135, **199**, 230
    coordinate, 144
    definitive, 122
    descriptive, 122
    evaluative, 122
    predicative, **121**, **229**
    superlative, 135, **199**
adjective phrase, 112, 113, 116, 118, 226, 233
    attributive, 230, 231, 232, 233
    predicative, 230
adverb, **50**, 111, 114, 123, 124, 151, 154, 169, 173, 174, 177, 185, 188, 191, 222, **224**, 225, 230
    comparative, 225
    superlative, 225
adverb phrase, 39, **50**, 112, 113, 115, 123, **124**, 125, 229, 230, 231
advice, 221

ambiguity, 15, 63–64, 139, 157–61, 164, 165
    modal, 63
    temporal, 64, 159
amount, monetary, 78
apostrophe, 149, 153, 190
appositive, **143**
archaic language, 57, 58
article, 111, 154, **197**
assertion, 220, 222
Associated Press Stylebook, *75*, 137
association, 47
attribute, 30, 47, 96, 97, 98, 155, 167, 168
attributive adjective, **121**, 122, **229**
attributive adjective phrase, 230, 231, 232, 233
Australian Government Style Manual, 122, 137, 154
Australian usage, 75, 76
auxiliary, 214, 216
bare form, *205*
base form, 125, **205**, 207, 208, 209, 210, 216, 217, 227, 228, 229
belief, 219, 220
bibliography, 86, *109*
BPMN, 99
bracket. *See* square bracket
breadcrumb, 102
bulleted list, 32, 33, 40, 42, 43, **68**, 138, 139, 140, 141, 145
Business Case, **91**
Business Glossary, 45, 46, 50, 51, 89, 100, **105**

business information model, **95**, 97
business language, 93
business rule specification, **100**
business rules, 30
button, 102
buzz phrase, 60
buzzword, 58, 59
Canadian Press Stylebook, 137
capacity, 218
capitalization, 26, 73, 153–55, 188
caption, 29, 42, 145
cardinal number, 133, 197
Change Request, 89, **103**
character style, 29
checkbox, 102
Chicago Manual of Style, 87
circuitous argument, 13
citation, 26, 86
clause, 39, 41, **113–18**, *120*, 127, 128, 223, 224, 225, 231
collaboration tool, 90
collective noun, 130
colon, 77, 85, 140, 141, 145, *146*, 147, 152, 153, 188
column, 30, 47, 96, 97, 98, 167
comma, 78, 79, 114, 117, 122, 127, 139, 142, 151, 152, 178, 187, 232, 233
    Oxford. *See* comma, serial
    parenthetical, 178
    serial, 137
comma splice, *144*, 179
comment, **34**
common noun, 189, 197
communication, 11
comparative adjective, 113, 121, 135, **199**, 230
comparative adverb, 225
complement, **116**, 120, 200
compound adjective, 110, 150, 191, **198**
compound noun, 41, 110, 121, 141, 154, 190, 191
compound preposition, 110

compound verb, 218, 219
compound word, 110
conceptual data model, 46
conclusion, 219
conditional clause, 120
conditional situation, 220
conjunction, 39, 111, 114, 120, 126, 127, 128, 129, 144, 154, 173, 174, 179, 185, 188, 204
    coordinating, 142, 145, 146, **223**
    logical, 231, 233
    subordinating, 114, 119, 167, **223**
constraint, 30, 96, 97
continuous tense. *See* progressive tense
Contract, *53*, *70*, 77, 89, **91**, 220
contraction, **66**, 149
contranym, **65**
controlled natural language, **100**
coordinate adjective, 144
coordinating conjunction, 142, 145, 146, **223**
count noun, **131**, 132, 133
countable noun. *See* count noun
cross-reference, 32, 70, 73, 85
currency symbol, 78
dangling modifier, 161
dash, 76, 147, 153
    em dash, **147**
    en dash, **147**
data model diagram, 98
data modeling standard, **105**
data naming standard, **106**
data specification, 23, 30, 31, **95**
data vault, 106
database, 168
database design standard, **105**
database management system, 168
date, 75, 147, 187
date picker, 102
decimal point, 79, 85
declarative sentence, **114**, 141
default language, 28
default present form, 205

defining clause, 143
definite article, 165
definition, 24, 48, **69**, 105, *109*
demonstrative determiner, 52, **197**
demonstrative pronoun, **201**, 207, 208, 210
dependent clause, 39, **114**, 123, 142, 223
    finite, **114**
descriptive approach, 118
determiner, 111, 112, 118, 126, 132, 133, 165, 167, 173, **197**, 224, 226
    demonstrative, 52, **197**
    distributive, **197**
    interrogative, **197**
    possessive, 52, **197**
diagram, 83, 109
    activity, 99
    data model, 98
    wireframe, **102**
dictionary, 14
digital online identifier, 87
direct object, 115, 116, 121, 123
direct question, 221
distributive determiner, **197**
document layout, **41–44**
document lifecycle, 89
document lifespan, 89
document structure, **30–32**
document version, 89, 90
double negative, 64
dropdown list, 102
ellipsis
    omission of repeated content, **40**, 41, *148*
    symbol, 72, 148
em dash, **147**
email, 107
emphasis, 44, 149
en dash, 79, **147**
English
    Australia, 183
    British Commonwealth, 18, 183
    Canada, 183

European Union, 18, 183
Ireland, 18, 183
New Zealand, 183
South Africa, 183
UK, 17, **183–88**
US, 17, **183–88**
entity. *See* entity class
entity class, 30, 31, 47, 70, 84, 95, 98, 155, 167, 172
entity-relationship model, 47
exclamation mark, 151
Executive Summary, *31*
expectation, 221
fewer, 132, 167
field, 48, 167, 168
finite clause, **113**, 114, 119
finite dependent clause, **114**
finite verb phrase, 112, 113, 115, 119, 225, 227
flat file, 48
focus. *See* comment
font, 29, 43, 44
    sans serif, 43, 44
    serif, 43
footer, 29, *109*
footnote, 29, *109*
foreign key, 47, 96, 97, 105
foreign plural, 192, 193
formal register, 25
French, 56
front matter, 29, 86, **88**, *109*
full stop. *See* period
functional requirement, **95**
future perfect tense, **211**
gender, 53
gerund, 110, 111, *190*, **192**, 196
gerundive, 111, *191*, **198**, 199
glossary, 25, 45, 46, 69, 70, 71, 145
grammar checking, 14
head word, 225, 226, 228, 229, 230, 231
header, 29, *109*

heading, 31, 42, 43, 55, 85, *109*, 142, 145, 153, 154
    table, 44
headline language, 61
hierarchic list, 68
homonym, 93
hyphen, 76, 79, 148, 150, 153, 154, 188, 190
hyphenation, 188
hypothesis, 220
icon, 102
identifier, numeric, **82**
idiom, 204, 222
imperative mood, 107, 115, 215, **216**
imperative sentence, **114**, 141
impersonal pronoun, 52, **200**
impossibility, 218
inability, 218
indefinite article, 140
indefinite pronoun, 190, **201**, 202
indent, left, 43, 44
indenting, 29
independent clause, 40, **114**, **115**, 142, 144, 145, 146, 147, 179, 223, 227
index, *109*
indicative mood, 107, 215
indirect object, 115, **116**, 121
indirect question, 164, 221
ineffective communication, 15
ineffective writing, 12
inference, 222
infinitive, 113, 135, 175, 204, 205, 207, 216, 223
infinitive phrase, 112, 115, 116, 124, 129, 226, 228, 229, 230
inflection, 112, 189
informal register, 26
information, numeric, **74–83**
informational component, 102
initialism, **72**, 74, 141
initials, 49
inline series, 40, **67**, 138, 139, 146, 147
input control, 102

International Organization for Standardization, 55, 235
interrogative, 216
interrogative determiner, **197**
interrogative mood, 120, 215, 217
interrogative pronoun, **201**
interrogative sentence, **114**, 151
intransitive verb, 115, **116**
irregular plural, 193
irregular verb, 205
ISO. *See* International Organization for Standardization
ISO 4217, 78
justification, **42**, 43, 44
language
    archaic, 57, 58
    default, 28
    headline, 61
    sales and marketing, 62
Latin, 56, *193*
left indent, 43, 44
less, 132, 167
line spacing, 29, 41, 42, 44
line style, 83
line weight, 83
linking clause, 54
linking phrase, **36**, 50, 54
list
    bulleted, 32, 33, 40, 42, 43, **68**, 138, 139, 140, 141, 145
    hierarchic, 68
    numbered, 32, 33, 40, 42, 43, **68**, 138, 139, 140, 141, 145
list box, 102
logical conjunction, 231, 233
logical data model, **96**, 97
logical operator, 203
lowercase, 77
main clause, 39, 142
main verb, 214, 217, 218, 221
mass noun, 130, **131**, 132, 133, 195

measurement, 132
measurement unit, **80–82**, 150
meeting minutes, **104**
message, 107
message box, 102
metadata, 88, 98
misplaced modifier, 162
modal, 55, 111, 124, 204, 205, 214, 215, 216,
  218, 220, 221, 227, 228
  ambiguous, 63
modal window, 102
monetary amount, 78
mood, **215–17**
mutating plural, 192
name, **48–50**, 149, 153
  personal, 188
narrative flow, **34–37**
NASA, 55
navigational component, 102
negation, **214**
negative prepositional phrase, 120
negative, double, 64
New Oxford Style Manual, 137
new page, 44
nominalization, **46**
nonbreaking space, **77**, 78, **80**, 81
noncountable noun. *See* mass noun
nondefining clause, 143
nonfinite clause, **113**, **114**
nonfinite verb phrase, 128, 167, 226, **228–29**
nonfunctional requirement, **95**
nonrestrictive relative clause, **117**, 169, 201
notification, 102
noun, 63, 111, 112, 114, 134, 150, 154, 169,
  173, 188, **189–97**, 202, 203, 205, 222, 226
  collective, 130
  common, 189, 197
  count, 133
  mass, 130, 133
  plural, 129, 130, 132, 133, 164, 174, 205, 207,
    208, 210

proper, 189, **196**, 197
singular, 53, 129, 130, 132, 133, 164, 190,
  205, 207, 210
noun chain, **66**
noun phrase, 37, 45, 46, 50, 82, 85, 100, **112**,
  113, 115, 116, 117, 118, 121, 123, 126, 127,
  131, 138, *143*, 149, 152, 157, 158, 162, 164,
  169, 173, 178, 199, 200, 201, **226**, *227*, 230,
  231
  plural, 118, 131, 164, 200
  possessive, 118
  singular, 200
number, 150
  cardinal, 133, 197
  ordinal, 75, **82**, 111, 150, **198**, 199
numbered list, 32, 33, 40, 42, 43, **68**, 138, 139,
  140, 141, 145
numeral, 74, 75, 76, 78, 79, 80
numeric identifier, **82**
numeric information, **74–83**
object, 117, 120, 124, 133, 165, 200, 223
object class, 47, 70, 98, 167
object class model, 47
object-relational database, 47
obligation, 55, 219, 220
oblique, 149, 153
operating system, 48
ordinal number, 75, **82**, 111, 150, **198**, 199
ornament, 83, 84
Oxford comma. *See* serial comma
pagination, 102
paragraph style, 29, 44
parenthesis, 146, 147, 153, 157
parenthetical comma, 178
parenthetical expression, 142, 147
participial phrase, 112, 113, 226, 230
  past, 112
  present, 112
participle, 50, 150, 151, 232
  past, 111, 198
  present, **198**

passive voice, 62, 136, 200, **214**
past participial phrase, 112, 229, 231
past participle, 111, 112, 113, 198, **205**, 208, 209, 211, 214, 227, 228, 229
past perfect tense, **211**
percentage, 80
perfect tense, **211**
period, 74, 76, 77, 85, 140, 141, 146, 151, 152, 184, 187, 188
permission, 219
personal name, 188
personal pronoun, **199**
   object form, 133
   subject form, 133
phrasal verb, 110, 111, **123**, 174, 191, **222**
phrase, 113, **225–33**
physical data model, **96**, 97
placename, 50, 148
Plain English, **37**
plain form, *205*
Plain Writing Act, 38, 55
plural, 165, 191, **192–96**
   foreign, 192, 193
   irregular, 193
   mutating, 192
   regular, 194, 195
   unmarked, 194
plural noun, 129, 130, 132, 133, 164, 174, 205, 207, 208, 210
plural noun phrase, 118, 131, 164
plural subject, 164
plural verb, 130, 131, 164
possessive determiner, 52, **197**
possessive form, 141, 149, 190, 202
possessive noun phrase, 118
possessive pronoun, **201**
possessive suffix, 190
possibility, 218, 219
post-relational database, 47
predicate, 150, *227*
predicative adjective, **121**, **229**
predicative adjective phrase, 230
preference, 221
preferred pronoun, 53
prefix, 150, 151
preposition, 111, 113, 117, 121, 123, 133, 134, 136, 154, 169, 173, 174, 188, 191, 200, **202**, *203*, 214, 222, 231
   beneficiary, 203
   causative, 203
   comparative, 203
   locational, 203
   perspective, 203
   possessive, 203
   temporal, 203
prepositional phrase, 101, 112, 113, 115, 118, 123, 126, 157, 158, 224, 226, 229, 230, 231
   negative, 120
prescriptive approach, 118, 119
present form, 227
present participial phrase, 112, 115, 128, 228, 231
present participle, 113, **198**, **205**, 207, 208, 212, 227, 228
present perfect tense, 129, **211**
present tense, 124
primary auxiliary, 111
primary key, 47, 96, 106, 168
process specification, **99**
product review, 89, 91, **92**, 93
progress bar, 102
Progress Report, 89, **104**
progressive tense, 129, **212**, 217
prohibition, 56, 219
Project Proposal, 31, **91**
pronoun, 52, 111, 112, 115, 116, 121, 127, 130, 133, 134, 154, 157, 188, **199**, 203, 205
   demonstrative, **201**, 207, 208, 210
   gender-neutral singular, *210*
   impersonal, 52, **200**
   indefinite, 190, **201**, 202
   interrogative, **201**

personal, 133, **199**
possessive, **201**
preferred, 53
reciprocal, **201**
reflexive, **201**
relative, **201**
proper noun, 110, 130, 189, **196**, 197
proposition, 222
punctuation, 26, 29, 72, 73, 85, 139, 141–53, 152, 153, 178, 179, 183, 187
quantifier, **197**
quantity, 78
question
   direct, 221
   indirect, 221
question mark, 151, 152
quotation, 147
quotation mark, 148, 151, 152, 153, 187
quoted material, 71, 142, 145, 148, 149, 151, 152
radio button, 102
readability, 33, 45
reciprocal pronoun, **201**
recommendations document, 30, 89, 91, **92**, 93
record, 47, 48, 167, 168
redundancy, 65
reflexive pronoun, **201**
register, **25**
regular plural, 194, 195
relational database, 47
relationship, 47, 83, 96, 97
relative clause, 112, 117, 144, 159, 201, 226
   nonrestrictive, **117**, 169, 201
   restrictive, 101, **117**, 118, 169, 197, 201
relative pronoun, **201**
Release Notice, 23, 89, **103**
Request for Tenders, 89, **90**, 91
requirement, 55, 90, 93, 98
   atomic, 93
   functional, **95**
   nonfunctional, **95**

Requirements Specification, 23, 89, **93**
restrictive relative clause, 101, **117**, 118, 169, 197, 201
row, 47, 167
run-on sentence, 179
sales and marketing language, 62
sans serif font, 43, 44
search field, 102
section, 30, 85
semicolon, 146, 152
semi-modal verb, 220–21
sentence, **109**
sentence case, 153, 154
sentence clarity, **32–34**
sentence length, 32, 38, 47
sentence structure, 13, 16
sentence stub, 138, 139
sequencing, 31
serial comma, 137
series, **67**, 134, 138, 143, 170
   inline, 40, **67**, 138, 139, 146, 147
serif font, 43
simple future tense, **210**
simple past form, **205**, 206, 208, 209, 211, 227
simple past tense, 124, **211**, **218**
simple present tense, 129, **210**, **211**, 218, 219
singular noun, 53, 129, 130, 132, 133, 164, 190, 205, 207, 210
singular subject, 165
singular verb, 130, 131, 164
slash. *See* oblique
slider, 102
small capitals, 77
software specification, 89, **95–103**
solidus. *See* oblique
space, 80, 152, 153, 190, 191
   nonbreaking, **77**, 78, **80**, 81
spacing, 43
   line, 29, 41, 42, 44
   vertical, 29, 41, 42, 44
spelling, 28, 183, 184

split infinitive, 125, 135
spreadsheet, 97, 100
SQL, 96
square bracket, 71, 147, 153
Standard Operating Procedures, 89, **107**, 151, 216
standard register, 26
star schema, 106
statement of fact, 54
statement of opinion, 54
stative verb, **212**
style
    character, 29
    paragraph, 29, 44
style guide, **26**, 42, 57, 72, 73, 74, 76, 77, 79, 87, 130, 141, 148, *152*, 154, 188, 209, 235
    Associated Press Stylebook, *75*, 137
    Australian Government Style Manual, 122, 137, 154
    Canadian Press Stylebook, 137
    Chicago Manual of Style, 87
    New Oxford Style Manual, 137
    UK, 188
subclass, 47
subject, **35**, 40, 41, 100, 101, 114, 115, 117, 118, 120, 126, 127, 133, 134, 136, 144, 161, 164, 178, 200, 201, 213, 214, 215, 216
subject area, 31, 98, 155
subjunctive mood, 215, **217**
subordinate clause, 114
subordinating conjunction, 114, 119, 167, **223**
subsection, 31, 85
subtype, 47
superclass, 47
superlative adjective, 135, **199**
superlative adverb, 225
supertype, 47
surname, 151
synonym, 47, 65, 93, 105
table, 30, 42, 44, 76, 96, 97, 98, 109, 167
table heading, 44

tag, 102
technical standard, 30, 31, 89, **105**
technical term, 24, 46, 69
template, 28
temporal ambiguity, 159
Tender, 89, **90**, 91
tense, **210–13**, 232
    future continuous, **212**
    future perfect, **211**
    future perfect continuous, **212**
    past perfect, **211**
    past perfect continuous, **212**
    perfect, **211**
    present, 124
    present continuous, **212**
    present perfect, 129, 211
    present perfect continuous, **212**
    progressive, 129, **212**, 217
    simple future, **210**
    simple past, 124, **211**, 216, **218**
    simple past continuous, **212**
    simple present, 129, **210**, 211, 216, 218, 219
term overload, 46, 168
text field, 102
text string, 148
theme. *See* topic
third person present form, **205**, 206
time of day, 76, 141, 145, 147
time picker, 102
time zone, 77
time, ambiguous, 64
title case, 153, 154, **188**
tooltip, 102
topic, **34**
transitive verb, **116**, 123
UK convention, 149, 151, **183–88**
UK English, **183–88**
UK publication, 75
UK rules, 154
UK style guide, 77, 188
UK terminology, 141

UK usage, 17, *46*, 75, 76, 77, *122*, 141, 142, 150, 152, **183–88**
unit, measurement, **80–82**, 150
unmarked plural, 194
uppercase, 77
US convention, 17, 149, **183–88**
US English, **183–88**
US rules, 154
US style guide, 137, 151
US usage, 17, 48, 75, 76, 77, *122*, 141, 142, 143, 150, 152, **183–88**
user guide. *See* user manual
user interface, 48
user interface specification, **102**
user interface standard, **106**
user manual, 27, 53, 89, **106**, 151, 216
verb, 111, 112, 113, 114, 115, 123, 134, 144, 154, 164, 169, 188, 198, 200, 202, 204–23, 224
    intransitive, 115
    irregular, 205
    main, 214, 217, 218, 221
    phrasal, 110, 111, **123**, 174, 191, **222**
    plural, 130, 131, 164
    semi-modal, 220–21
    singular, 130, 131, 164
    stative, **212**
verb form
    bare form, *205*
    base form, 125, **205**, 207, 208, 209, 210, 216, 217, 227, 228, 229
    default present form, 205
    infinitive, 113, 135, 175, 204, 205, 207, 216, 223
    past participle, **205**, 208, 209, 211, 214, 227, 228, 229
    plain form, *205*
    present form, 227
    present participle, **205**, 207, 208, 212, 227, 228
    simple past form, **205**, 206, 208, 209, 211, 227
    third person present form, **205**, 206
verb phrase, 45, 100, 112, 115, 120, 121, 123, 124, 135, 138, 150, 173, *227*, 232
    finite, 112, 113, 115, 119, 225, 227
    nonfinite, 128, 167, **228–29**
verbosity, 16
vertical spacing, 29, 41, 42, 44
vocabulary
    UK, 183
    US, 183
weasel word, 54, **62**
window, 102
wireframe, **102**
word class, **110**, 189
word order, **120–26**, 161–64
XML, 96
XML schema, 96, 106

www.ingramcontent.com/pod-product-compliance
Lightning Source LLC
Chambersburg PA
CBHW081428070526
44586CB00020B/2521